Culture, Poverty, and Education

Culture, Poverty, and Education

What's Happening in Today's Schools?

Michele Wages, PhD

ROWMAN & LITTLEFIELD
Lanham • Boulder • New York • London

Published by Rowman & Littlefield
A wholly owned subsidiary of The Rowman & Littlefield Publishing Group, Inc.
4501 Forbes Boulevard, Suite 200, Lanham, Maryland 20706
www.rowman.com

Unit A, Whitacre Mews, 26-34 Stannary Street, London SE11 4AB, United Kingdom

British Library Cataloguing in Publication Information Available

Library of Congress Cataloging-in-Publication Data

Wages, Michele, 1965– author.
Culture, poverty, and education : what's happening in today's schools? /
Dr. Michele Wages.
  pages cm
Includes bibliographical references.
ISBN 978-1-4758-2011-9 (cloth : alk. paper) — ISBN 978-1-4758-2012-6
(pbk. : alk. paper) — ISBN 978-1-4758-2013-3 (electronic) 1. Education—
Social aspects—United States. 2. Students with social disabilities—United States.
3. Poor—Education—United States. 4. Poor—United States. 5. Poverty—United States.
6. Education—Parent participation—United States. 7. Cultural awareness—United
States. 8. Multicultural education—United States. I. Title.
LC191.4.W344 2015
306.43—dc23   2015024832

Printed in the United States of America

Contents

Preface

Even though the requirement from the federal government to raise test scores of economically disadvantaged children has occurred, there is still a disconnect for today's teachers because there has been no increase in support systems to address the issue put into place. In 2013, a UNICEF report ranked the United States as having the second-highest relative child poverty rate in the developed world. At just 20 percent, that is one in five American children living in poverty, which is one of the greatest threats to a child's well-being.

Many of the students now sitting in our college classrooms will continue on to become teachers. Sadly, they will graduate without ever taking a course that exposes them to the reality of poverty or, more importantly, prepares them to work in this environment. Teacher-preparation programs, including graduate degrees, should require courses that provide an overview of poverty and methods of working with this population.

In the 2011 academic year, Mississippi had the highest portion of students from low-income families, at 71 percent. Oklahoma was second at 61 percent followed by Texas at 50 percent and South Dakota at 37 percent. Children from low-income families represent a majority of public school students in all but two of the fifteen southern states. Although southern states have seen rising numbers of poor students for the past decade, the trend has spread west in 2011 to include rapidly increasing levels of poverty among students in California, Nevada, Oregon, and New Mexico (Layton, 2013).

The economic definition of poverty is typically based on income measures, with the absolute poverty line calculated as the food expenditure necessary to meet dietary recommendations, supplemented by a small allowance for nonfood goods. In 2012, the U.S. Census declared the poverty line for a family of four (two adults and two children under the age of eighteen) to be less than $23,492 in earnings.

We must never equate poverty with dysfunction. Many people from low-socioeconomic-status backgrounds are very successful, well-rounded individuals making important contributions to society. Nevertheless, it must be acknowledged that living in a low-socioeconomic environment can present several major challenges especially for children.

Understanding the relationship between poverty, class, and education for decades has been framed through studies on the behavior and culture of poor students and their families. Educators are caught up in the history of classism and are often guilty of buying into the mindset that includes the implementation of activities and strategies for working with parents in poverty or students in poverty that leads them to believe in the need to "fix" the poor instead of eliminating the inequities that oppress them. So it is not just one or the other; nature or nurture, poor or not poor. Poverty is a potential outcome for all of us.

Most changes in education, including the rise of standardized testing, holding teachers accountable for their students' academic performance, and rewriting math and reading standards don't address poverty.

This book is intended to not only discuss five myths about the culture of poverty and its effects on education but also provide some resources on alternatives for educators to better address this growing barrier to student achievement in today's schools.

Introduction

In 2012, more than 26 million eighteen- to sixty-four-year-old adults lived under the poverty line; about 15 million of them did not have a job during the year. Is this the economy's fault, or are personal choices to blame? Certainly, personal choices play a role in our lives, and some individuals make poor choices that contribute to future problems.

There are however, significant systemic barriers that feed the cycle of poverty. Poverty occurs for many reasons. Someone can find themselves in tough financial circumstances because of their own actions, because of the actions of other people in their family, or because of factors beyond their control. Poverty status can often depend upon decisions made by family members, such as whether to apply for government services or seek employment (Mayers, 1997).

Teachers are baffled with statements like:

"These kids are smart, I know they are, but . . ."

- they don't care about school;
- they are unmotivated (lazy);
- their parents don't care; and
- these kids are unprepared to learn.

The truth is that many children living in poverty are bright, motivated individuals who could overcome their circumstances, given the opportunity. When Band-Aid approaches fail, it can result in increased frustration for everyone. The consequence of this frustration is widespread stereotyping and the formation of a blame-the-victim mentality.

In 1961, a book by Oscar Lewis entitled *The Children of Sanchez* coined the term "culture of poverty," based on his studies of small Mexican communities. In it, Lewis states:

- Poor people develop distinct subcultural values that enable them to survive poverty but disadvantage their children in school.
- As individuals, people feel helpless and disempowered.
- By the age of six or seven, children have absorbed the values of their culture and cannot take advantage of opportunities that may lie ahead.

In short, Lewis argued that low-income Mexicans and Puerto Ricans self-perpetuated a culture of poverty that included violence, an inability to defer gratification, and political apathy. In other words, poor people are poor because of deficiencies based on stereotypes.

The term *culture* is often used to explain away many of today's problems in education. Educators often use it as a code word when talking about differences and/or deviance. In reality however, the concept of "culture of poverty" is actually nonexistent. The truth is that differences in behaviors and values among poor people are just as great as those between poor and wealthy people.

Culture is randomly and regularly used to explain everything. So while teacher-education students learn nothing about culture, they use it with authority as one of the primary explanations for everything from school failure to problems with behavior management and discipline.

Unfortunately, the majority of preservice teachers take a series of foundation courses on the history, philosophy, and sociology of education, but the anthropology of education rarely appears in their teacher-education coursework.

The education system is often considered to be the great equalizer among people of diverse backgrounds. Most school mission statements or district goals include something about all students being treated equally and being provided the same opportunities to succeed. The reality, according to the U.S. Department of Education in 2011, is that low-income students continue to be disadvantaged, lacking a quality education with rigorous courses to prepare them for college and the services that will help them post–high school.

The truth is that poor children live in environments with social conditions over which they have little control. It is not their choice where they live, whether their parent may be unemployed or disabled, or to be born into poverty. They often are overwhelmed with the feeling of wanting to escape the environment and do better, but they feel they have no control over the nature and quality of their lives. As educators, it is our responsibility to show children they can be agents (individuals that intentionally make things happen through their actions) and show them they can be a part of their self-development and take responsibility for their learning, personal development, and achievement (Bandura, 2001).

People in poverty have the right to do what it takes to survive. They are not fundamentally different from the privileged class and should not be treated as second-class citizens. In a country that brags of its level playing field and claims to value its children and their education above all else, how have we allowed such a massive failure to fester among our own?

Children who come from generations of poverty or those who find themselves there because of life's circumstances still dream, have hopes, and want to achieve. Poverty does not mean a person cannot succeed. Children who live in poverty can meet high expectations and standards and know when teachers are watering down curriculum or oversimplifying instruction for them.

WHAT IS POVERTY?

Poverty has many definitions; for the purpose of this book, it refers to persons with income less than that deemed sufficient to purchase basic needs—food, shelter, clothing, and other essentials. The reality is that poverty is complex and does not mean the same thing for all people. A child living in poverty lacks goods and services considered essential to human well-being. Devising an operational measure of poverty that accurately reflects a child's well-being in terms of his or her economic resources is complex. A child's well-being depends on both how many resources are available to his or her family and how many adults in the family allocate these resources among family members. Resources include the goods and services purchased for the child by family, those provided by the government, and those produced within the family.

Six Types of Poverty

1. **Absolute Poverty:** It is the extreme kind of poverty, involving the chronic lack of basic food, clean water, health care, and housing. People in absolute poverty tend to struggle to live, and they experience a lot of child deaths from preventable diseases. This type is usually long-term in nature and often handed down to children from generations before them. Examples would be persons who have to use surface water (river or streams) for drinking, lack access to a toilet facility, live in a place where there are more than four people in a room, and lack access to schools or any type of media.

2. **Relative Poverty:** In relation to other members and families in society, these people lack the minimum amount of income needed to maintain the average standard of living in the society in which they live. People are said to be impoverished if they cannot keep up with the standard of living as determined by society.

3. **Situational Poverty:** These families are poor due to some adversities like earthquakes, floods, or serious illnesses. Sometimes people can help themselves out of the situation quickly if they are given a bit of assistance. Many times the cause of their situation is some unfortunate event.

4. **Generational or Chronic Poverty:** This is poverty handed down to individuals and families from generations before them (at least two generations have been born in poverty). In this type, there is usually no escape, as people are trapped in its cause and have no access to tools that will help them get out of it.

5. **Urban Poverty:** This type occurs in metropolitan areas with a population of at least fifty thousand. The urban people deal with a complex aggregate of chronic and acute stressors (including crowding, violence, and noise) and are dependent on often inadequate large-city services.

6. **Rural Poverty:** This type occurs in nonmetropolitan areas with a population below fifty thousand. There are more single-guardian households, and families often have less access to services, support for disabilities, and quality educational opportunities. Programs to encourage transition from welfare to work are problematic in remote rural areas where job opportunities are few.

Chapter 1

Three Theoretical Models on the Culture of Poverty

In a country well governed, poverty is something to be ashamed of.
In a country badly governed, wealth is something to be ashamed of.

—Confucius

The fact that students from disadvantaged households perform less well in school, on average, than their peers from more advantaged backgrounds is seldom disputed. Unfortunately, those who make the policies choose to avoid the problem instead of facing it head-on using reasoning that allows them to focus on things they can control instead of ways to change the backgrounds of students.

In attempts to explain the widespread underachievement among students of color and students from lower-socioeconomic status in schools, educators have historically targeted the root of the problem as the students, their families, and communities. This perspective overlooks the main causes of oppression by localizing the issue within individuals and/or their communities. There are three theoretical models that attempt to explain the achievement gap across cultures and socioeconomic status.

1. CULTURAL DEFICIT MODEL

Since the mid-1900s, cultural deficiency has been used in academic discourse and various fields with the aliases of "culture of poverty" or "culture of deprivation," It stems from the negative belief that poor performance and widespread underachievement is attributed by the student's socioeconomic status and familial origin. The research in this theory blames the students

themselves for their underachievement by latching on and referring to negative stereotypes often affiliated with the population. Interestingly enough, the
school itself is not held accountable and is absolved from its responsibilities
to educate appropriately and this charge is shifted almost entirely to students
and families (Irizarry, 2009).

This theory basically feeds off negative stereotypes directly linked to the
student's ability to work and to perform compared to systemically marginal-
ized people (Irizarry, 2009). It states that children of low-income status and
minority race lack exposure to certain cultural models that are congruent with
school success.

According to this perspective, students of color and low-income backgrounds often enter school with a lack of "cultural capital" (Bourdieu, 1997),
cultural assets that are affirmed by schools and often shared by school agents,
and therefore considered valuable. Also, a popular assumption exists that
these families do not value education in the same ways as students from
middle- and upper-class families who, according to this theory, are more
likely to do well in school because they possess more cultural capital.

By directing the causes of a student's underachievement within student
groups and communities, the cultural deficit model allows policy makers to
avoid examining institutional barriers (i.e., school funding, racial and ethnic
segregation) that can also potentially influence student achievement. It also
fails to acknowledge the relationships between school practices, the socio-
political factors that shape these efforts and student outcomes. Schools must
acknowledge the social and cultural capital present in communities of color
and those of the poor (Gonzalez, 2005).

A cultural deficit perspective is comprised of two parts:

- the attribution of an individual's achievement to cultural factors alone,
  without regard to individual characteristics, and
- the attribution of failure to a cultural group. In other words, a cultural-
  deficit perspective is a view that individuals from some cultural groups lack
  the ability to achieve just because of their cultural background.

In short, it is the perspective that minority group members are different
because their culture is deficient in important ways from the dominant majority group. It fails to address these realities:

- Since 1970, the dollar has lost 80 percent of its purchasing power. Those in
  the lower or middle class, on a fixed income, lose the most.
- Marriage rates have dropped by one half in the last fifty years, yet cohabi-
  tating married couples who have children after age twenty-one, reduce their
  chances of poverty to under 5 percent.

- Schools rarely prepare kids for life in the real world by teaching job-ready life skills (relationship skills, effort building, executive function skills, positive attitudes, and money/finance skills). If you are educated with good life skills and married, your odds of being poor are under 2 percent.

2. CULTURAL DIFFERENCE MODEL

The second theoretical model, the *cultural difference* model, points to differences in values, expectations, languages, and communication patterns between teachers and students—or between schools and families—as a source of difficulty for ethnic-minority students. The underlying theory is that the social organization, learning formats and expectations, communication patterns, and sociolinguistic environments of schools are incongruent with the cultural patterns of different ethnic groups and therefore limit the opportunities for student success.

Where teachers and students are unable to fully understand each other is the interpersonal communication level that some researchers focus on as to the important differences that exist. These communicative differences have many levels, including formal language (e.g., English versus Spanish), conventions for interacting (e.g., distance between speakers, acceptable physical contact, and turn-taking rules), preferences for rhetorical style (e.g., the use of emotion in persuasion), and storytelling patterns.

The differences between social worlds have also been studied, and the results indicate that it can be difficult for ethnic-minority students to negotiate between home and school. For example, where U.S. public schooling tends to encourage independence, with competition and rewards for individual achievement, some ethnic groups may tend to encourage interdependence among members, with rewards for collaborative effort. The practice of socialization often varies across ethnic groups in that, for example, the parenting styles acceptable within one ethnic group may vary significantly from the parenting styles valued by schools and educators.

The parents' role in education may also differ across ethnic groups, so that while some teachers expect active parent involvement at school, parents' conceptions of involvement may be altogether different. With parenting go parenting practices that also vary. Some may focus on social and observational learning, which involves stronger visual than auditory information processing. Others may expect more traditional methods of lecturing and rote memorization.

Some researchers believe that the cultural difference model presumes ethnic differences to be inherently problematic, but, in fact, it is in how people act on these perceptions of difference that is an important source of difficulty for minority students. These researchers often practice a cultural-process approach while focusing on social interactions. The barriers to school success are determined by examining how students, teachers, and parents understand the patterns of language use and socialization.

Regardless of the stance taken, the cultural difference model has made important contributions to understanding the relationship between ethnicity and school achievement because it points out that children from different ethnic groups vary in cultural patterns, some of which are important for today's educators to understand.

3. SOCIOSYSTEMIC MODEL

A third theoretical model, which can be termed *sociosystemic*, moves outside the classroom in an effort to identify the social, economic, and political forces that contribute to the achievement gap. Research has uncovered how differences in perceived economic opportunity affect the level of school engagement for ethnic-minority students. When for instance, students' families, peers, and community members have beliefs that economic and social opportunities are limited, regardless of school achievement, students are far less likely to engage in meaningful ways with formal educational activities. These beliefs may lead to a youth's active resistance to school or a "disidentification" with schooling overall (i.e., when students are apathetic or disaffected toward schooling) (Kyllonen and Gitomer, 2002).

Where school achievement varies according to the conditions of one's minority status, some studies have identified patterns of differences within ethnic-minority groups. Those individuals who immigrated for improved economic opportunity are known as *voluntary minority groups* and often do better in school than members of involuntary minority groups (those whose residency was forced: slavery or colonization). The sociosystemic model has also been used in research to identify schools as the places where societal pressure to assimilate is often resisted. We all have experience with the pressures of high school, and the desire to fit in and be liked. The hard truth is that student peer groups link school achievement to the acceptance or rejection of various identities.

From the cultural difference model, schools and teachers are encouraged to make better use of the knowledge and practices of diverse cultures and to form home-school connections. The various forms of multicultural education also derive from a basic cultural difference model, as do some bilingual education programs. Also included in this model are recent efforts to develop theories and practices of *culturally relevant pedagogy,* an approach to teaching that modifies both curriculum and communication to reflect the diverse cultural practices of students. The cultural difference model appears to decrease the pressure on children to conform to mainstream culture standards, yet to increase the pressure on teachers and schools to transform their practices to better reflect the diversity that is present around them.

For those with a sociosystemic perspective, repairing the achievement gap demands a commitment to an ongoing examination of the social and political systems, along with direct action to counter systemic bias. Few formal policies or programs with this model exist, although *critical theory* and *critical pedagogy* are actively promoted within this perspective. Critical theory seeks to make systemic injustice visible and critical pedagogy encourages teachers and students to understand and contend with stereotyping, racism, sexism, and other forms of prejudice.

Because of the tremendous variation within any ethnic group, it would be inappropriate to make generalizations about the needs and abilities of any individual student based solely on his or her membership in a given ethnic group. That said, there is no doubt that variation does exist along several lines, and educators should be aware of this. Perhaps most important of all, members of the teaching and learning community ought to be reflective of their own perceptions and actions with respect to all learners. Schools and teachers are encouraged to make better use of the knowledge and practices of diverse culture and form home-school connections.

It must be recognized that just as schools themselves vary, so do the students within them. Schools are the spaces where a great deal of a youth's development occurs, and on multiple levels, including academic achievement, identity, and social competence. In the end, ethnicity and culture must become part of the face of education in order to reflect and better serve our youth as they encounter an increasingly diverse world.

This book was not written to preach as to which model is superior. The models are simply offered so that the reader can have a better understanding of philosophies and viewpoints on this subject. This book does address some of the myths about the culture of poverty and the effects on a child's education. However, it barely touches the surface of the traumatic, unequal treatment of the impoverished in our public school system. It also provides a few strategies that today's teachers can add to their tool belt to better prepare them to show our future achievable options in finding a brighter path to walk.

Chapter 2

Myth Number 1

Poor People Are Unmotivated and Have Weak Work Ethic?

No family gets rich from earning the minimum wage. In fact, the current minimum wage does not even lift a family out of poverty.

—Jon Corzine

The astonishing truth is that poverty is not a lifestyle by choice—people don't long to be poor. In America, we have homeless PhDs and a tremendous number of middle-class workers on food stamps. In all reality, there are more people in poverty than we are willing to admit.

According to Wilson (1997), poor people do not have weaker work ethics or lower levels of motivation than wealthier people. Although poor people are often stereotyped as lazy, 83 percent of children from low-income families have at least one employed parent. Close to 60 percent have at least one parent who works full-time and year-round (National Center for Children in Poverty, 2004). In fact, the severe shortage of living-wage jobs means that many poor adults spend more hours working each week than their wealthier counterparts.

The National Student Campaign Against Hunger and Homelessness reported that in 2012, the national poverty rate rose to 13.2 percent of the population. In addition, 3.5 million people were forced to sleep in parks, under bridges, in shelters or cars. The combination of the high cost of living, low-wage jobs, and high unemployment rates only exacerbate these problems and force countless Americans to choose between eating, shelter, and other expenses. Money devoted to food is typically the first to be sacrificed. More often than not, people will make fixed payments first, such as rent and utilities, rather than pay for food. The average food stamps benefit breaks down to approximately four dollars a day. The number of Americans on food stamps now exceeds the population of Spain (Worstall, 2013).

Whether the government admits to it or not, the working poor is one of the fastest growing segments of the U.S. population. At this point (2014) approximately one out of every four part-time workers in America is living below the poverty line. For the most part, many middle-class families do not worry about food or transportation or whether walking to school involves crossing a gang boundary. They have shelter and health care when they need it. If a crisis hits, they have savings to fall back on or at least access to credit on reasonable terms. It is a wonder that many middle-class adults can even imagine being poor.

You may be surprised to learn that the homeless population includes people from all walks of life:

- 23 percent are military veterans;
- 30 percent have experienced domestic violence;
- 20 to 25 percent suffer from mental illness;
- 35 percent are families with children; and
- 25 percent are children under the age of eighteen.

According to the National Student Campaign Against Hunger and Homelessness, the main causes of poverty are as follows:

- Lack of affordable housing—individuals need to earn wages of $15.37 an hour, nearly three times the current minimum wage, to afford a two-bedroom apartment at the average fair-market rent.
- Low incomes—most cannot afford food AND shelter. The minimum wage has continually decreased in value since the late 1960s.
- Lack of affordable medical care—this can cost a family up to $8,000 a year; a sudden illness, chronic disease or accident can be financially devastating.
- Political factors—many cuts in federal assistance for housing and social services, cuts in programs like temporary assistance for needy families have attributed to people staying poor.
- Social and medical factors—mental illness, drug addiction, and alcoholism exacerbate situations of poverty and put people at greater risk of homelessness.

The 2014 U.S. poverty guidelines reveal that the cutoff for poverty in a two-person household is $15,730 per year (Miller, 2015). Many who are currently in poverty were born and raised in poverty and spend their efforts working from a very young age to survive. Because of facing these challenges, they rarely meet financial obligations or attend college. This limits their options for employment because often the jobs they do qualify for do not take into consideration the need for childcare in work schedules. The number of children living on two dollars a day or less in the United States has grown to 2.8 million (Worstall, 2013). It is also true that many people don't apply for professional jobs simply because they can't afford to look nice enough to hold them.

Lack of work ethic? The reality is that often minimum wage jobs require labor-intensive tasks that leave the employee physically drained every day. The mountain of work grows as the person completes tasks, and with the realization of management that the person is capable and willing to bear a heavy workload. This causes the employee to realize their best work is never to be shown as it leads to more work, while others get away with minimum tasks for the same pay. The employee soon realizes this and slowly pulls back, resulting in being viewed by management as one of the "lazies."

The truth of the matter is that the employee chooses to sacrifice their work output for their own health and well-being. The tough decision of going against conventional wisdom and not work as hard is seen as evidence of laziness and a lack of desire to work, but it is actually learned helplessness.

In 2007, 6.4 percent of adults who lived under the poverty line and did not work in the previous year said it was because they could not find a job. As of 2012, the figure had more than doubled to 13.5 percent. Given there are three unemployed Americans for every job opening, the claim of not being able to find a job as the number one reason for poverty shouldn't be much of a surprise. The poor people choosing not to work aren't necessarily doing so out of laziness but because they have other obligations; they are trying to take care of relatives, they are ill, or they are attempting to make their way through school. Taking away their meal ticket won't fix any of these problems.

In 2010, the Department of Agriculture reported that 7 percent of those sixteen years and older who did work some or all of the year were in poverty. They also reported that 30 percent of households receiving food stamps had earnings and 41 percent of food-aid beneficiaries lived in a household with earnings from a job. In addition, nearly a quarter (21.8 percent) of nonelderly adult food-assistance recipients were employed.

Poverty is often associated with minority status. Many Americans believe that African Americans and Hispanics make up the largest portion of the poverty population. In truth, of the one in seven American head of households receiving food assistance, whites account for 35.7 percent, 22 percent are African American and 10 percent are Hispanic.

In 2013, 46.6 percent of food stamp recipients were children, and another 7.9 percent were elderly; this does not even include those who were not children or elderly but had a disability that prevented or limited work. These figures are astounding and reveal that the statement "just get a job" is an inappropriate solution for upward of half of all food-benefit recipients (National Center for Children in Poverty, 2012).

In addition, the National Center for Children in Poverty also reported that 64 percent of those in poverty were unable to work due to being too young or too old, due to a disability of some kind, or because they simply could not find a job. In 2010, more than 10.6 million people in poverty were part of the working poor (part of the labor force for at least twenty-seven weeks) and 2.6 million of them worked full-time and still remained under the poverty line.

In 2012, the Bureau of Labor Statistics reported that 1.57 million Americans earned the minimum wage of $7.25 an hour. Over 60 percent of minimum wage earners were in retail, or in leisure and hospitality, which includes hotels and restaurants. In an article entitled "11 Jobs Where an Honest Day's Work Earns You Poverty," L. S. Parramore (2014) lists the following jobs that hardworking people hold and, as a reward, earn minimum wage or, sadly, less than minimum wage:

- Airport workers—most cabin cleaners, baggage handlers, and other cleaning crews earn $8.00 an hour with no health benefits.
- Big-box store employees (Home Depot, Walmart, Target).
- Casino workers—dealers and drink servers are either at minimum wage or just a notch above with many having to put up with drunk, grabby customers, long hours on their feet and breathing in clouds of smoke.
- Fast-food workers have a median income of $8.94 an hour (nonmanagerial) and the average worker's age is twenty-eight.
- Grandma's aide—home health aides, personal care aides and certified nursing assistants receive minimum wage and are hardly ever paid overtime.
- Fishing industry workers, whose duties include operating equipment, pulling lines in and preserving the catch, have some of the most dangerous jobs in America. Minimum wage laws do not apply to crew-member jobs. Often wages are based on a share of the harvest or on a per day rate.
- Truckers are paid by the mile in an outdated-type payment known as *piecework*. The driver does not get paid unless the wheels are moving and therefore is not paid for downtime such as when refueling or unloading.
- Construction and extraction workers—day laborers and helpers are among the lowest paid workers on construction sites. The median hourly wage for day laborers is $10.00. The work is unstable and insecure and often includes working with hazardous materials and tasks such as building scaffolding and being near explosives. Few receive health benefits.
- Nail salon workers earn minimum wage, and many do not receive overtime and are required to work through their lunch. They are also exposed to chemicals that may not have been tested for safety.
- Farm workers are paid according to the amount of work they do, in piecework fashion, such as by the number of buckets of berries they pick. These

workers perform back-breaking tasks for less than the equivalent of minimum wage.
• Housekeepers and cleaners are supposed to receive minimum wage but live-in housekeepers often can't even expect overtime pay or basic labor protection. Maids in motels and bargain hotels often do not receive the tips customers leave and earn an average of $7.81 an hour.

The bottom line is that there are lazy poor people, just as there are lazy rich people. Does this mean there is always an excuse for being poor? Of course not. There is however, ample evidence to conclude that laziness plays a limited role in poverty in comparison to the multitude of other relevant factors at play.

Chapter 3

Myth Number 2

Poor Parents Are Uninvolved in Their Children's Learning Largely Because They Do Not Value Education?

Ninety-eight percent of parents, regardless of socioeconomic status, want their children to achieve better than they have.

—Michigan Department of Education

Low-income parents hold the same attitudes about education that wealthy parents do (Compton-Lilly, 2004). Most are less likely to attend school functions or volunteer in their children's classrooms (National Center for Education Statistics, 2005)—not because they care less about education, but because they have less access to school involvement than their wealthier peers. They are more likely to work multiple jobs, to work evenings, to have jobs without paid leave and to be unable to afford childcare and public transportation. As a whole, the education system fails to take these considerations into account and does not value the involvement of poor families as much as it values the involvement of other families

The problem, according to a Pew study, is that only 11 percent of the people from these circumstances got a college diploma. Even for people in exceptional cases, attaining a college degree gives them a better chance of making it out of poverty—but it is no guarantee, let alone a solution to poverty. Nearly half a million people working for minimum wage have an associate or bachelor's degree, according to an analysis of Bureau of Labor Statistics data. The total student-loan debt in the United States surpassed 1 trillion dollars, with students graduating with an average debt of nearly thirty thousand dollars. This means getting a college degree already puts one in debt before their first job interview.

Regardless of how many people manage to get a college degree, if the jobs that are being created for them don't pay a living wage, much less an income once assumed for the college graduate, it becomes a moot point. Don't misunderstand me, higher education should be a human right, and its expansion would benefit all of society. The fact remains, however, that the belief that better schools and more education mean less poverty is false.

The reality is that students with strong academic abilities and supportive parents are basically guaranteed to graduate. Remedial students who benefit from involved proactive parents are likely to earn a diploma. Conversely, dedicated students who possess good academic skills can possibly graduate, despite living with uninvolved parents or in a dysfunctional home environment. However, students with poor academic skills who also suffer from a lack of parental involvement or support have virtually no chance of graduating from high school (Okun, 2008).

In many instances, poverty causes parents to be so wrapped up in their own problems (overworked, overstressed, meeting financial demands) that they are blind to how uninvolved they are in their children's lives or are unable to provide the emotional support most children require. It is often the case in poor households that emotions are at a premium. Overworked, overstressed parents tend to be authoritarian with children because that is how they were raised. This results in the normal formation of a solid, healthy relationship with their children to be nonexistent.

In addition, it is often the case that children in low-socioeconomic households are home alone to fend for themselves and their younger siblings while their parents work long hours. This results in the children spending less time playing outdoors and more time watching TV, with after-school activities rarely being encouraged (U.S. Census Bureau, 2000). Unfortunately, children won't get the model of how to develop proper emotions or respond appropriately to others by watching cartoons.

Children of low-income parents are typically half as likely to be tracked down in the neighborhood or have their whereabouts known by their parents (Evans, 2004). These parents also frequently do not know the names of their children's teachers or friends. As far as serving on school committees, 27 percent of children living below the poverty line had parents serve on a school committee as compared to 45 percent of those living above the poverty line.

In reality, it is more likely that these parents don't know how to help their children, and the current system provides them with few opportunities to be involved in ways that fit into the realities of their lives. It is often the case that for people in poverty, education has a lack of meaning because of the relevancy to their lives. They attended school for such reasons as "it was the law" (Beegle, Dehejia, and Gatti, 2006). For many, school was a source of discomfort in their lives; it was full of stress and unhappiness and a place they felt they did not belong (p. 69). Limited conversations with their parents, in which educational expectations, issues related to success in school, or higher education were the topics, was usually the norm during their formative years. The cause of their lessened involvement is not attributed to devaluing education, but rather to parents' limited frame of reference for discussing educational aspirations beyond their own experiences.

America's Promise Alliance documents that in our nation's fifty largest cities, only 50 percent of high school students graduate. They go on to state that by the age of seventeen, urban dropouts are relegated to a life on the fringes (higher rates of poverty, incarceration, unemployment, government assistance, health problems, etc.). Few will debate that a better educated work force is more likely to enjoy higher earnings. But the truth is that education by itself is an insufficient antipoverty tool. Yes, poor people absolutely need more education and skill training, but they also need an economic context wherein they can realize the economic returns from their improved human capital (Bernstein, 2007).

Think about it; would there really be less poverty if everyone was better educated? The reality is that the resources to end poverty exist in abundance and generally aren't found inside a school building. The highest paying careers do generally require a college degree, whereas jobs open to high school graduates that once paid a living wage are being eliminated or turned into low-wage work.

The fact of the matter is that one's wage, or lack of, is not a barrier to parental involvement. As teachers, if a student is not experiencing success, we want to be able to reach out to parents. The reality today, however, is that educators presume that having impoverished parents come to school will result in the same results as having middle-class parents come.

Today's educators need to consider the parents' perceptions of involvement when attempting to understand and increase their participation. According to Feldman (2003), if parents do not show interest in how their children are doing, if they ignore messages that teachers send home, or if they fail to come to conferences, teachers are likely to feel helpless, while parents may feel they are doing the best they can.

Parent-teacher conferences are often misunderstood by both parties. Whereas teachers want to get right to the point, parents from poverty have a tendency to "beat around the bush" first. When teachers redirect the conversation, usually due to time constraints, and get right to the point, impoverished parents tend to view it as being rude and uncaring. In poverty, children are viewed as possessions that must be protected at all costs (Payne, 2008). To avoid this defense mechanism, teachers need to take the time to begin to build a relationships with the parents. As a result, more cooperation will be gained from them as well as more acceptance as the teacher begins to teach the hidden rules of schools and the middle class to them. Educators need to take the time to show a parent that they care and explain to them the reasons why it is important for their children to stay in school.

Parent involvement has been linked to indicators of student academic success (Fan and Chen, 2001) when schools support parents' involvement in their children's learning; regardless of the families' income, education level, or ethnic background, children are more likely to earn higher grades and test scores, and enroll in higher level programs (Christenson, 2004).

In order to encourage participation nonconventional, culturally responsive activities need to be implemented that encourage parents to be involved in their child's education (Delgado-Gaitan, 2004). Some examples of these include workshops that are flexible and motivate parents to help their children at home. Including activities that help families come together and build relationships between school and parents need to be priority.

Lee and Bowen (2006) stated that parents' perception of their children's education varies and includes different activities such as attending parent-teacher conferences or programs that feature their children and other students, or participating in volunteer activities. As an educator, understanding cultural views and individual perceptions of what parent involvement entails is key (Trotman, 2001). It is possible that parents perceive themselves as participating in their child's education by being involved in the school setting as a teacher's aide or tutor, by attending field trips or assisting with fundraising activities. Others perceive involvement as including the following activities:

- providing their children with a place to study
- helping their children with homework
- monitoring their child's degree of television watching
- setting curfew for their children.

An important marker in educational development has been the reading proficiency by fourth grade. This is the stage in development where students start reading to learn as opposed to learning to read. Unfortunately, with the implementation of No Child Left Behind, traditional developmental stages in learning have been discarded and the curriculum that used to be taught in one grade is now being taught at earlier grade levels. In today's schools, kids who can't read by the end of first grade are often already in such deep reading trouble that they don't catch up.

The bottom line is that today's educators have to respect the skills low-socioeconomic families have developed in order to survive in a dangerous environment that is chaotic and hostile, and recognize the effort they put forth to provide for their children and other family members.

Once this respect is established, it will be possible to achieve many other things that will aid in motivating students and their parents away from generational poverty.

The truth of the matter is that poor people, demonstrating impressive resilience, value education just as much as wealthy people (Compton-Lilly, 2004; Grenfell and James, 1998), despite the fact that they often experience schools as unwelcoming and inequitable.

Some evidence includes:

- In a study of low-income urban families, Compton-Lilly (2004) found that parents, overwhelmingly, have high educational expectations for their children and expect their children's teachers to have equally high expectations for them, particularly in reading;
- In their study focusing on low-income African American parents, Cirecie West-Olatunji and her colleagues (2010) found that they regularly reached out to their children's schools and stressed the importance of education to their children;
- Similarly, Patricia Jennings (2004), in her study on how women on welfare respond to the "culture of poverty" stereotype, found that single mothers voraciously valued and sought out educational opportunities for themselves, both as a way to secure living-wage work and as an opportunity to model the importance of school to their children;
- Based on their study of 234 low-income parents and guardians, Kathryn Drummond and Deborah Stipek (2004) found that they worked tirelessly to support their children's intellectual development;
- During an ethnographic study of a racially diverse group of low-income families, Guofang Li (2010) found that parents, including those who were not English proficient, used a variety of strategies to bolster their children's literacy development;
- A recent study shows, contrasting popular perception, that poor families invest just as much time as their wealthier counterparts exploring school options for their children (Grady, Bielick, and Aud, 2010); and
- Using data from the more than twenty thousand families that participated in the Early Childhood Longitudinal Study, Carey Cooper and her colleagues (2010) found, quite simply, that "poor parents reported engaging their children in home-learning activities as often as nonpoor parents" (p. 876).

Chapter 4

Myth Number 3

Poor People Are Linguistically Deficient?

> All children come to school with extraordinary linguistic, cultural and
> intellectual resources, just not the same resources.
>
> —Hart and Risley, 1995

One of the most persistent myths about language-minority children is that
their first language and culture present deficits or deficiencies to be overcome
by the school. All people, regardless of the languages and language varieties they speak, use a full continuum of language registers (Boomer, Dworin,
May, and Semingson, 2008). What's more, linguists have known for decades
that all language varieties are highly structured with complex grammatical
rules (Gee, 2004; Miller, Cho, and Bracey, 2005). What often are assumed
to be deficient varieties of English are no less sophisticated than so-called
standard English.

It is a well-accepted notion that children from impoverished families enter
school linguistically deprived with reduced or less complex vocabularies
than their wealthier peers. It also appears to be part of the common sense of
education reform that this condition is the fault of the families' "cultures" and
the lack of value on learning. This view is largely based on a single study by
Hart and Risley (1995) of a few dozen economically diverse families in the
Kansas City area.

The high level of reading failure among children living in poverty is often
linked to the claim that poor children lack the rich and varied vocabulary
needed to succeed in school (Labbo, Love, and Ryan, 2007). These perceived linguistic deficiencies are blamed on the parents and credited to their
lack of sufficient provision of a rich language-learning environment for their
children.

Fortunately, there is good reason not to criticize. When teachers assume that language is a marker of intelligence, the stereotype that poor people are also language poor negatively affects their assessments of low-income students' performance (Grant, Oka, and Baker, 2009). This well-accepted stereotype is built upon two shaky assumptions, according to Gorski (2008): (1) poor children do not enter school with the volume or type of vocabulary they need to succeed (and this is a reflection of parent disinterest in education), and (2) the use of particular variations of English reflect inferior language capabilities.

The truth is, there is no evidence that the discrepancy in reading skills is connected to a language-use deficiency or that it reflects parent disinterest in education (Flessa, 2007). The facts are that low-income families often have limited education, which reduces their ability to provide a stimulating environment in their home. The children's linguistic environments tend to be limited to the use of language that is dominated by commands and simple structures, with little explanation and elaboration. Communication also tends to be full of high incidences of negative comments.

One example lies in the belief that talking to babies is important or necessary. Some parents with low income and limited educational opportunities are not aware that children who are rarely spoken to or are not given much language stimulation during their first year of life will suffer a dramatic reduction of linguistic and cognitive development from very early on.

It is well known that, in general, children with poor phonemic awareness fall further behind as they go through school. As this book presents, the poverty rate for children is excessively high, and therefore the two are related. In addition, children with low or nonexistent levels of literacy in their home languages tend to have difficulty with formal schooling tasks. For many of these children, school is a culture shock. It is for this reason that these children present special challenges for the school system because they do not qualify as having language-learning disabilities; they simply come from environments where language stimulation and literacy are not readily available.

Shanks (2012) found that by the age of three, poor children already have half the vocabulary of higher-income children. Shanks also points out that in an additional study, children in high-risk social and economic environments can start in the top 25 percent academically at the age of four, but fall to the bottom by the time they are in high school. In most cases, many children start out school eager to learn and wanting to achieve. Unfortunately as the effects of poverty beat them down, they are left with the perception that no one cares about their efforts, and because their basic needs are not being met with each passing grade, they start to become less engaged in school and search for other ways to survive. I agree with Shanks that this is tragic and unacceptable.

Language can be defined as a means of communication that shapes cultural and personal identity and socializes one into a cultural group (Gollnick and Chinn, 2006). Language can be composed of nonverbal and verbal, as well as oral and written, components. It is impossible to separate language and culture because, simply, one cannot be defined without the other. In order to participate fully in a culture, one must learn that culture's language. Conversely, in order to be fluent in a language, one must learn the culture that the language represents (Terry and Irving, 2010, p. 115).

Another common language stereotype is that children from poor families might speak as if speaking to their sister or a close friend (informal registry), whereas their middle-class and wealthier peers speak as if on a job interview (formal registry). However, like other forms of code switching—the ways we modify behavior based on the context in which we find ourselves—all people use a broad range of language registers (Brizuela, Andersen, and Stallings, 1999; Edwards, 1976), regardless of the variety of language they speak.

Berstein (2007) characterized middle-class children as using an elaborated "code" compromised by the values of order, rationality, stability, and control of emotion. Their dialect contained many relational and abstract terms that were viewed as suitable for complex intellectual activity. In contrast, the "restricted code" used by lower-class children included short, simple, syntactically incomplete sentences, with few subordinates, limited adjectives and adverbs, and little evidence of concrete descriptive phrases. This impoverished language was argued to be much less useful in communicating the complex ideas and relationships required for the abstract-reasoning tasks in today's academic school work (Ginsburg and Opper, 1969). This results in an overshadowing view of working-class families and parents as being highly nonverbal, impulsive, authoritarian, and dysfunctional, and ties in neatly to Lewis's list of cultural traits that people living in a culture of poverty allegedly share.

Gorski (2008) suggests that evidence exists that indicates oral vocabulary is not as closely related to reading and writing vocabularies as many may think. He goes on to state that, in reality, a child's oral linguistics is not an indicator of their ability to learn to read. Reading is new to all kids, regardless of how well they might speak. "As with other social identities and oppressions, the notion of a language 'norm' is handed down by the privileged classes, ensuring that their norm is understood as 'the norm'" (Speicher and Bielanski, 2000).

Another component that educators may not take into account is a poor family's inadequate access to health care and the numerous implications that can have. One example: when children are frequently sick and medical care cannot be afforded, these children are absent from school for longer periods of time, resulting in gaps in academic information. Oftentimes, when these children do attend they are unable to fully concentrate and have little motivation to participate in activities. Also, children who do not see doctors frequently may have untreated ear infections that can be detrimental to auditory discrimination and processing skills, language development, and articulation.

When a situation occurs where a negative stereotype could be applied, people of poverty know what people could think and therefore know that anything they do that fits into the stereotype will most likely be taken as confirming it. They also know that, for that reason, they could be judged accordingly (Steele, 2010, p. 5). This weighs on their consciousness and can affect the student's cognitive performance and emotional well-being.

Gorski (2008) states that, due to the deficit theory, many teachers are defining students by their weaknesses rather than their strengths and we (Americans) are much less likely to support authentic antipoverty policy and programs. The truth be told, it is this theory that justifies privileges and advantages that students from the upper class receive and the disadvantages that students from the poor working class receive, and unless educators start thinking outside of the theory components, the cycle where "we ignore the ways in which our society cheats the poor student out of opportunities that their wealthier peers take for granted" will continue (Gorski, 2008, pp. 34–35).

Chapter 5

Myth Number 4

Poor People Tend to Abuse Drugs and Alcohol?

Poverty is a veil that obscures the face of greatness. An appeal is a mask covering the face of tribulation.

—Khalil Gibran

Which comes first, poverty or addiction, is much like the question about the chicken and the egg. Poor people are no more likely than their wealthier counterparts to abuse alcohol or drugs. Although drug sales are more visible in poor neighborhoods, drug use is equally distributed across poor, middle-class and wealthy communities (Saxe et al., 2002). Chen, Sheth, Krejci, and Wallace (2003) found that alcohol consumption is significantly higher among white upper-middle-class high school students than among poor black high school students. Their findings support a history of research showing that alcohol abuse is far more prevalent among wealthy people than among poor people (Diala, Muntaner, and Wairah, 2004). In other words, considering alcohol and illicit drugs together, wealthy people are now more likely than poor people to be substance abusers.

Contrary to beliefs, some stereotypes that are associated commonly with poor people, such as the propensity for alcohol abuse, are more true of wealthy people than they are of poor people (Galea, Ahern, Tracy, and Vlahov, 2007). Think about it; how often do we hear, "No wonder so many rich kids don't do well in college, their parents are alcoholics?" Drug addiction and alcoholism do not discriminate based on economic status, social standing, education level, or any ethnicity. Unfortunately, however, those from prestigious backgrounds are often able to avoid being reported in detrimental statistics.

Economic status does not determine whether a person becomes an addict. No research exists that identifies a single factor that determines whether someone trying drugs, alcohol, or cigarettes will become addicted to them. The truth is, it is a mixture of biology, environmental factors, developmental stage, social environment, and even gender and ethnicity. Sharing in the belief that overcoming poverty or addiction is a simple as "willpower" or "wanting it enough" is an American myth that needs to be abandoned. It is a grand notion, but the flip side to that argument is that you are solely responsible if you don't succeed in life and with that comes intense pressure of accountability.

It is reported that around the world, alcohol use and addiction are positively linked with income; in other words, the higher somebody's income, the more likely he or she is to use alcohol or to be an alcoholic (Degenhardt et al., 2008). A study from Monitoring the Future (2008), reported that regardless of age, there is equal distribution of alcohol and drug use across socioeconomic status. I am not denying that there is a link between poverty and addiction, but there is much more to poverty than just addiction. I do believe, however, that most people in poverty are not addicted to heroin, crack, or alcohol but are just struggling to make ends meet.

The fact of the matter is that poverty can be a contributing factor to drug abuse, especially in a situation where someone uses drugs or drinks to "feel better" about life. Addiction is not necessarily a result of poverty, but it can cause poverty as a person slips deeper into the addiction lifestyle and throws his or her life away. In coping with the dangerous environment they live in or dealing with financial stresses, physical or emotional abuse can be the trigger for an impoverished person to abuse drugs or alcohol. Impoverished neighborhoods often provide the perfect atmosphere for drug and alcohol accessibility and often entice people into actually selling drugs with the hope of overcoming poverty.

Poor people smoke, although it is expensive, because it is often their best option. Often working multiple jobs leaves them exhausted and the nicotine serves as a stimulant. When they cannot go one more step, they smoke and can go on for another hour. In addition, coping with daily stresses often leaves them feeling beaten down and incapable of accomplishing one more thing. In this case, they smoke and feel better, if only for a minute. In most cases, their feeling of relaxation is the only one they are allowed. They are aware of the health dangers and know it is not a good decision to smoke, but it is all they have access to and often the only means they have to avoid exploding or collapsing.

Community and Family Medicine at Duke University conducted a study that ran from 1986 to 2009. Their findings reported that children who grow up in poverty were more likely than wealthier children to smoke cigarettes but were less likely to binge drink and no more prone to marijuana usage. The study also concluded that neither wealth nor poverty appeared to influence marijuana use, although positive parenting did reduce the use of this drug.

Parents who were nurturing and accepting, in fact, diminished the likelihood of young people using any of the substances.

Drug use and addiction have no single cause, but risk factors for drug use include poverty. Marks (2009) states that there are many risk factors associated with drug and alcohol abuse. These include:

- childhood experiences
- genes
- mental illness
- psychological factors
- low status
- low-skilled jobs
- unstable family and interpersonal relationships
- high arrest rates
- high incidence of mental disorders
- poor physical health
- high mortality rates
- dropping out of school
- illegitimacy

In reality, even people who are not suffering from poverty can embody these risk factors. It is unfortunate that many people who are poor become entrenched in the lifestyle that often leads to and reinforces incarceration, exposure to law enforcement, poor health outcomes, and homelessness. This leads the public to believe that poor people abuse drugs and alcohol, a belief that is potentially biased because of skewed reporting.

One of the many differences income makes on alcohol and drug dependency is in the quality of the substance abused. For those not suffering from poverty can afford to buy alcohol that is higher quality or drugs that are more pure than those impoverished people. Higher wage earners also have access to clean needles and other drug equipment that helps reduce their risk of infection or disease. Those who are poor often do not have these choices. They find themselves consuming low-quality alcohol that may have health consequences, and the drugs they can afford to purchase may be cut with dangerous adulterants or be toxic.

The myth of welfare recipients spending their benefits on drugs is just that—a myth. When it comes to addiction, people caught in the cycle of poverty who also suffer from substance abuse have an even harder time breaking out of the cycle and removing themselves from the harmful life they lead than those who are not poor. It has also been recorded that parents who suffer from addiction to drugs or alcohol pass along to their children a higher risk of also suffering from this disease.

"Perhaps the greatest impact of poverty on the life of a drug user is how it can make prevention and treatment efforts inaccessible to that person" (Beaufils, 2014). The U.S. Census Bureau (2000), states that of approximately one out of every six (48 million) Americans living in poverty, only 3.7 million are in need of treatment for drug use or alcohol addiction, but only a quarter of those actually get the treatment they need.

The fact of the matter is that some people can overcome poverty or addiction or both, but some people can't. Much of this is due to the wide variety of ways our society and our brains are fundamentally structured, not the amount of money one has or does not have. And that, like losing anyone to addiction, is a tragedy.

Chapter 6

Myth Number 5

*Poverty Has Little Lasting
Impact on Children?*

Anyone who has ever struggled with poverty knows how extremely
expensive it is to be poor.

—James A. Baldwin

EFFECTS OF POVERTY ON CHILD DEVELOPMENT

Poverty can impede children's ability to learn and can contribute to social,
emotional, and behavioral problems. Poverty also can contribute to poor
physical and mental health. Risks are greatest for children who experience
poverty when they are young and/or experience deep and persistent poverty
(National Center for Children in Poverty, 2012).

A child living in poverty must first overcome enormous barriers to meeting life's basic needs before being able to make the best life for themselves.
Their desire to learn and their determination take a back seat to their ability
to tackle these barriers (Gorski, 2007).

Brady-Smith, Fauth, and Brooks-Gunn (1999) state that the effects of
poverty seem to be the strongest the earlier in a child's life it occurs, when
it is constant and causes the child to live well below the poverty threshold.
Brooks-Gunn and Duncan (1997) found that there are at least five pathways
that poverty may influence child development:

1. child health and nutrition;
2. parent mental health and affective interaction;
3. provision of a stimulating home environment;
4. school and childcare quality; and
5. neighborhood conditions.

In 2009, the National Center of Family Homelessness reported that poverty was the single greatest threat to a child's well-being. Due to lack of nutrition as well as physical-stimulation and/or emotional-development deficits, children living in poverty are at a dangerously high risk for mental and physical disorders.

A family's living in poverty can result in a child having a poor diet and therefore be deficient in vitamins, particularly vitamin B, and have anemia, which can cause long-lasting neurological deficits when untreated. Due to poor housing conditions, lead poisoning is more common in children of poverty, and this can adversely impact brain function.

The Centers for Disease Control and Prevention (2012) estimated that 450,000 children between ages of one and five had enough lead in their blood to impair cognitive development. Asthma, another condition that is much more prevalent in low-income populations can also interfere with learning. Asthma has reached epidemic proportions among poor children in America, causing them to miss from twenty to forty days of school per year.

According to Mukherjee (2013), there are four ways that poverty hurts Americans' long-term health:

1. Poverty prevents Americans from buying healthy food. Many poor are forced (due to no transportation or physical disability) to patronize neighborhood bodegas or mini-marts that specialize in salty snacks and highly processed foods that lead to hypertension, obesity, and diabetes, instead of choosing fresh produce. In a 2009 U.S. Department of Agriculture report, it was found that 11.5 million Americans are both poor and live in low-income areas over a mile away from a supermarket that offers healthier food varieties.
2. Poor people are more likely to smoke. In a 2013 study conducted by Duke University School of Medicine, it was concluded that children who grow up in poverty are more likely to smoke cigarettes and may actually be predisposed to picking up this unhealthy habit. "Economic strains may shape an individual's capacity for self-control by diminishing opportunities for self-regulation or affecting important brain structures" (p. 1).
3. The poor live in regions with worse air quality. In 2013, the American Lung Association stated that poor people were more likely to live close to sources of pollution like industrial plants that emit harmful particles. They also reported that people in poverty suffer from medical problems that make air pollution even worse for their health. Children of poverty are more likely to live in high-pollution areas, with more exposure to mercury, lead, polychlorinated biphenyl's (PCBs), and smog, which influence health and learning and often impact behavior (Berliner, 2012).
4. Economic insecurity has devastating consequences for both physical and mental health. Hyman (2010) states that the mental stress of being

poor creates a food insecurity that promotes bingeing on cheap sugary, starchy, fatty calories in order to avoid hunger. A diet comprised primarily of these foods can cause high blood pressure, high cholesterol, and obesity as well as increase the chances of diabetes since long-term stress creates hormones that compromise the immune system and promote weight gain.

The neural systems of poor children develop differently from those of middle-class children, affecting language development and executive function, or the ability to plan, remember details, and pay attention in school. This can result in behavioral and emotional problems. Examples of behavioral problems may include impulsiveness, difficulty getting along with peers, aggression, attention-deficit/hyperactivity disorder (ADHD), and conduct disorder. Some examples of emotional problems may include feelings of anxiety, depression, and low self-esteem. It is also shocking to know that poor children can be up to two times more likely than nonpoor children to suffer from stunted growth, iron deficiency, and severe asthma. According to Driscoll and Nagel (2012), "A government study in 1996 also showed that poverty placed children at greater risk of dying before their first birthday than did a mother's smoking during pregnancy."

Children of poverty face great emotional trauma. Their emotional climate is often stressful and extremely depriving. This includes a lack of emotional nurturing that can result in aggressive or impulsive behavior or complete social withdrawal. Sadly, their emotional security and self-esteem are often lacking as they respond to their craving for attention and need to belong (Ciaccio, 2000).

Cognitive functioning can be impaired by these physical ailments and can lead to undiagnosed and untreated conditions that stunt learning, reduce ability to function, and lead to a lifetime of learning deficits. A 2001 study found that 50 percent of children living in poverty had vision deficiency that could be corrected, but their families could not afford the cost (Berliner, 2012).

Inadequate health care, lack of health insurance, and contaminated living space can cause children from economically disadvantaged families to suffer from preventable illnesses not experienced by their middle-class or wealthier peers. Children of poverty are also more likely to:

- experience hunger;
- be homeless;
- go without meals, shelter, and warmth;
- live in neighborhoods with unsafe levels of environmental pollutants;
- lack safe places to play; and
- lack safe water to drink and safe air to breathe.

In a 2013 report by the Child Poverty Action Group, it was found that by the age of sixteen, children receiving free school meals had attained 1.7 grades lower than other students, and by the end of primary school, free lunch recipients were estimated to be almost three terms behind their affluent peers.

High mobility rates present yet another hurdle for low-income students to overcome. If parents are unable to pay bills, they move more frequently, which often results in requiring children to change schools, sometimes several times a year. This results in students losing continuity of studies, relationships, and routines, and leads to them often falling behind in the curriculum. Children living in poverty have a high level of absenteeism or leave school all-together because they are more likely to have to work or care for family members.

Schooling is also impacted by the daily environmental stress that many poor children must cope with. The stress of a single-parent household can result in arbitrary discipline and reduce the frequency of positive family interactions for the impoverished child. Oftentimes their neighborhoods are riddled with crime and drugs with few positive role models present. As one can only imagine, these problems can breed behavior problems, and the chronic stress these children live in can adversely affect their concentration, memory, and consequently their ability to learn.

EFFECTS OF POVERTY ON EDUCATIONAL OUTCOMES

Whenever American students' test scores are publicized, an upheaval of dispute erupts. The fact is, however, that according to the Program for International Student Assessment (PISA) report (2012), American kids in very low poverty schools score as high or higher than anybody else on the planet (Strauss, 2011). Even though many low-income families often have limited education, reducing their ability to provide a responsive, stimulating environment for their children, their households do not usually sit idle, waiting for growth or program benefits to come their way. They cope by adopting strategies to address their difficult situations that tide them over until better times.

Student achievement is affected by poverty. That is not to say that reforms and efforts to improve teacher quality, modernize curriculum, and infuse technology into the classroom where it makes sense should not be pursued. But doing all of that while ignoring the conditions in which kids live is a big waste of time. The facts are, according to Brady-Smith, Fauth, and Brooks-Gunn (1999):

- More than one-third of low-income students begin kindergarten not ready for school.
- By the time these children reach fourth grade, 50 percent will not be at grade level in reading.
- In high school, the dropout rate for students from low-income families was 8.7 percent in 2008 compared to 2 percent from higher-income families (American Psychological Association, 2008).
- Thirty-two percent of the students who spend more than half their childhood in poverty do not graduate.
- Low-income students repeat grades at a rate of 28.8 percent compared to 14.1 percent of higher-income families.
- The percent of low-income students expelled or suspended from school is 11.9, compared to 6.1 percent of higher-income students.
- Low-income students are 1.4 times more likely to be identified as having a learning disability in elementary or high school.

According to the National Council for the Social Studies Professional (2013), "How much money a child's parents earned last year does not in itself impede learning. But poverty is a good proxy, sometimes, for lower-class status because it is so highly associated with Americans' overall beliefs on characteristics of that status" (p. 5). As the research cited within the pages of this book state, lower-class families have:

- lower parental-literacy levels;
- poorer health;
- less stable housing;
- more exposure to crime and other stresses;
- less access to quality early childhood experiences;
- less access to good after-school care;
- earlier childbearing;
- more frequent unwed childbearing;
- less security that comes from unstable employment; and
- more exposure to environmental toxins that diminish cognitive ability.

How can this reality NOT affect student achievement?

Each one of the above bullets predicts lower achievement for children, but none of these (including low income) in itself causes low achievement. It can be the case that lower-income families don't necessarily have all of these characteristics, but they are likely to have many of them (Rothstein, 2013). It is also important to take into account that the effects of poverty on the child increase with the duration of poverty and the extent of poverty.

Chapter 7

The Effects of Poverty on the Brain

Hope is necessary in every condition. The miseries of poverty, sickness and captivity would, without this comfort, be insupportable.

—William Samuel Johnson

A child's home life affects their educational growth, including language and vocabulary skills. A study published by the Association for Supervision and Curriculum Development (ASCD) found that children of higher income parents increased their vocabularies at twice the rate of children in poverty. Additionally, delays in brain development are 1.3 times more common in children who live below the poverty line nationally, according to the Connecticut Commission on Families. Overall, 5 percent of low-income children experience delays in brain development and 8.3 percent have learning disabilities, according to a study by Princeton University published in The Future of Our Children.

In general, we know that brains are built from the bottom up, with simple skills and circuits forming a foundation in early childhood for complex circuits and skills that are built later. Unfortunately, when children lack opportunities for positive serve-and-return interaction (when the responses from adults are sporadic, inappropriate, or missing entirely) their brain stimulation is greatly reduced, which prevents healthy brain development.

Past research has identified three factors in brain development:

1. the child's relationships
2. learning resources
3. stress

Being born into a poor household increases the chance of exhibiting psychological symptoms when compared to those being born to a nonpoor household. In 1993, a group of researchers started an eight-year longitudinal study of children in the Great Smoky Mountains, a range of peaks along the North Carolina-Tennessee border. One thousand, four hundred twenty children were recruited—25 percent Native American, 7.5 percent black and the rest white—and given psychiatric exams annually. Unsurprisingly, the children from poor families were found to have problems, about 60 percent more than their middle-class counterparts.

There are also near-term consequences of poverty on adult brains. For instance, the stress of poverty has the same effect on a person's cognitive ability as pulling an all-nighter every night, and can decrease a person's IQ by as much as 13 percent (Covert, 2013). A study at the Washington University School of Medicine associates poverty in early childhood with smaller brain volumes from ages six to twelve (Templeton, 2013). This type of problem can lead to chronic depression and degenerative brain disease.

Unfortunately, it is often the case that when poor children do not meet the diagnostic criteria for psychiatric disorders, they are still prescribed amphetamines. This exposes them to the side effects, which can include stunted growth and stimulant induced psychosis. Poverty takes its toll on health in a number of other critical ways. It prevents families from buying healthy foods, makes people more likely to smoke, which means they are more likely to live in areas with poor air quality and, more disturbing, often these health problems begin in the womb.

There are three main types of stress:

1. Positive stress: (which is short lived, like the stress experienced on the first day of school) actually helps a child develop coping skills and a healthy stress-response system.
2. Tolerable stress: like that experienced when a loved one dies, but is not damaging if a child has the buffering support of protective adult relationships.
3. Toxic stress: occurs in the absence of consistent supportive relationships and can lead to lifelong problems in learning behavior and both physical and mental health.

There are many circumstances that can trigger toxic stress, including poverty, exposure to violence, parental substance abuse, mental illness, and serious child maltreatment. The link between toxic stress and the long-term health outcomes of children of poverty cannot be excluded when medical personnel treat symptoms. Excessive exposure to toxic stress can disrupt the development of brain architecture, and children raised in poverty are much more likely to experience toxic stress than their nonpoor peers.

There are also other negative impacts from poverty. Children's brains, particularly in working memory can be impaired from the chronic stress of growing up in poverty. A study of veterans found that poverty is a bigger risk factor for mental illness than being exposed to warfare (Covert, 2013). The mental stress of being poor is also a major reason for why low-income people tend to have negative health outcomes like high blood pressure and cholesterol or elevated rates of obesity and diabetes.

The effects of chronic stress are as follows:

1. It creates emotional problems (Burgess et al., 1995).
2. It lowers IQ, reading scores (Delancy-Black et al., 2002).
3. It creates memory loss (Lupien et al., 2001).
4. It shortens dendrites (Cook and Wellman, 2004).
5. It causes neuron death (DeBellis, 2001).
6. It fosters inappropriate attachments (Schore, 2002).

The constant discharge of stress hormones that people in poverty experience causes immune responses of excess inflammation that often leads to of heart disease, hypertension, type 2 diabetes, autoimmune disease, gastrointestinal problems and depression, among many other problems linked to stress (Templeton, 2013).

By the age of fifty, individuals who have experienced poverty in childhood are 46 percent more likely to have asthma, 83 percent are more likely to have been diagnosed with diabetes, and 40 percent are more likely to have been diagnosed with heart disease in comparison to individuals whose incomes are 200 percent of the poverty line or greater (Coleman, 1990).

Long-lasting changes in the brain also occur in people who grow up in poverty. These changes harm emotional processing and can increase a child's odds of mental health problems. The neurological impacts of childhood poverty may even include higher mortality rates, according to a new study by scientists at the University of Denver Family and Child Neuroscience Lab (Pyke, 2013).

In this University of Denver study, negative images were used to study adults' emotional responses to negative images. The results showed that the portion of the group that grew up poor was less able to minimize their emotional reactions to the images than the other half of the group that was not raised poor. This lack of emotional processing ability can have serious consequences that can contribute to difficulties in regulating of emotions and future devastating health outcomes, including mental illness and high mortality and morbidity in adulthood.

Many children who grew up poor have impaired brain function as they enter adulthood, which was clearly seen in the MRI scan by researchers. Children who were poor at age nine had greater activity in the amygdala and less activity in the prefrontal cortex at age twenty-four, which is significant because these two regions of the brain play a critical role in how we detect threats and manage stress and emotions. These same patterns of "dysregulation" in the brain have been observed in people with depression, anxiety disorders, aggression, and post–traumatic stress disorders.

In a 2013 study conducted by Luby et al., it was concluded that early childhood exposure to poverty was associated with smaller white matter, cortical gray matter, and hippocampus (the part of the brain that plays an important role in the consolidation of information from short-term memory to long-term memory and spatial navigation) and the amygdala (almond-shaped group of nuclei that perform a primary role in the processing of memory, decision-making, and emotional reactions).

The fact of the matter is that there is an association between childhood poverty and health that extends into adulthood. Economic disadvantage in childhood has been linked to worse overall health status and higher rates of mortality in adulthood (Casey, 2005).

The studies cited in this chapter are only a small portion of the evidence existing that economic hardship has direct negative consequences on people that cannot be easily dismissed by simply telling people to try harder. Although tough for Americans to admit, poverty is more closely linked to mental illness than exposure to warfare, and those children who manage to survive poverty's mental health side effects face other health factors that may develop into permanent health damage.

So does poverty affect the brain? Poverty taxes the ability of parents to do all kinds of things, including caring for their children. The reality is that the developmental challenges children face in a home full of stressed adults may well influence the adults that they, themselves, become.

Chapter 8

The Culture of Classism

In the 21st century, I think the heroes will be the people who will improve the quality of life, fight poverty and introduce more sustainability.

—Bertrand Piccard

Manza and Sauder (2009) define *classism* as

differential treatment based on social class or perceived social class. Classism is the systematic oppression of subordinated class groups to advantage and strengthen the dominant class groups. It's the systematic assignment of characteristics of worth and ability based on social class.

That includes:

- individual attitudes and behaviors;
- systems of policies and practices that are set up to benefit the upper classes at the expense of the lower classes, resulting in drastic income and wealth inequality;
- the rationale that supports these systems and this unequal valuing; and
- the culture that perpetuates them.

The deficit theory is the most destructive tool in what is known as the "culture of classism." It is often referred to when one is talking about the deficit perspective in education and is composed of defining students by their weaknesses rather than focusing on their strengths (Collins, 1988). There are two main strategies that propagate this worldview based on deficit theories which are:

- drawing on well-established stereotypes; and
- ignoring systemic conditions such as inequitable access to high-quality schooling that supports the cycle of poverty.

If education is the all-proven pathway out of poverty, then why do some children achieve this goal while others do not? It is often the case that lower-income young people develop lower ideals and expectations for their higher education attainment than their nonpoor peers. It is thought that the claim that there is a "culture of poverty" that limits academic and vocational success of poorer people is based on a flawed theory of culture that ignores the rich language and experience possessed by children from all cultural and linguistic groups (González, 2005).

Often the conflict between schools and poor and minority children and their families is complicated by racism and classism. Families are often left feeling devalued when schools represent an Anglo-centric and middle-class viewpoint. Although this experience is more common to Spanish-speaking children, the issue is less one of language than of the context used socially, leaving these children, their families, and communities feeling undervalued. School often compromises second-language learners' potential by rejecting their language and culture, the celebration of which would result in higher self-confidence and self-esteem. This devaluing of poor and minority children provides mixed messages, which causes them to feel pressured in choosing between identifying with family and friends and disavowing the school, or embracing the school and facing emotional and social isolation. The result is that many young children opt for family and friends and become unwilling participants in school culture.

Blaming the poor for being poor does not open one's thinking up to the possibility of other, systemic explanations for poverty or school failure. There is, for example, no reason to wonder how impoverished curricula (Oakes, 2006), underresourced schools (Kozol, 1992), and an insufficiency of high-quality teachers in high-poverty schools (Olson, 2006) could limit the academic performance of many poor students. Nor is there any reason to consider how the conditions of poverty affect children's physical, emotional, and neurological development and day-to-day performance in school (Books, 2004).

"Most Americans do not easily embrace systemic explanations for academic failure. In our highly individualistic, meritocratic society, it is generally assumed that academic underachievement is evidence of personal failure" (Mills, 1959).

Until a dam is built to stop the steady stream of profits for the high-stakes testing companies, the educational politicians will continue to push through the endless harmful education policies that are tearing apart American's schools. The profession is starting to experience a rampant exit of teachers who are choosing to leave the profession, get fired, or be so beaten down from the daily demoralization and stress they endure while working under the tyrant known as accountability that is based on meaningless numbers (Berliner, 2012).

As educators and parents, the temptation of deficit ideology must be resisted and the problem of poverty needs to be placed where it is due, the cause of the disenfranchising of poor communities instead of blaming it on the communities themselves. This also means rejecting solutions to classism aimed at youth that are meant to "fix the poor people" rather than "fix the economic injustice."

The reality today in America is that class not only affects people at an economic level but also at an emotional one. Great pain has been caused by classist attitudes and by dividing people from one another while preventing individuals from accessing opportunities to achieve personal fulfillment or the means to survive.

Overcrowded and underresourced schools have denied poor youth many opportunities and often provide less rigorous curricula by focusing on skilling and drilling instead of broader and more in-depth concepts like their wealthier peers. These children of poverty also are left to carry the burden of disen-franchisement suffered by their family from a society that refuses to provide their parents or guardians with living-wage work or decent health care. This creates a double whammy of economic injustice.

Conflicts in how children have been taught to view the world can occur between home and school. The standards of behavior, qualities of interpersonal relationships, and the goals and objectives of education can also cause misinterpretations between communities and educators. These differences in expression can hide the common roots both views share. For example, "creativity" may show up in graffiti and "task persistence" may be demonstrated in playing video games, but neither predicts diligence and inventiveness in classroom activities (Bowman, 1994).

One such example is the fact that some cultures value physical aggression and "macho" behavior. These children often exhibit difficulty in their ability to suppress these behaviors in the school setting. Other children who were raised more conservatively may view open aggression at school as deeply threatening. All of these children, whether they tolerate high levels of aggressive behavior or do not, acquired their characteristics through the process of identification with the values and behavior of family and friends (Bowman, 1994).

Let me be clear, I am not stating whether high or low levels of aggression should be acceptable, I am simply emphasizing that acquiring such behavior is a normal accomplishment in some communities. Unfortunately, schools do not realize that in valuing low aggression in children, they are opening the door for cultural conflict for others who do not believe that lack of aggression can reflect competence and effectiveness.

Ogbu (1992) points out that the same types of prejudice and discrimination are not experienced by all groups. He notes that "involuntary" minorities (primarily African Americans, Native Americans, and some Hispanics) are exposed to a more pervasive and extensive exclusion from the mainstream than are other minorities. Because of this, they are more likely to avoid learning skills that are emphasized by the white middle class, due to the belief that their efforts will not result in the same opportunities that others who comply will receive. Consequently, oppositional practices that separate them from the mainstream are developed and often school achievement leads to the loss of peer affiliation and support (Bowman, 1994).

Every person belongs to a social class including the class their parents occupy. They are born into it and thrown into its culture. Educators need to avoid getting caught up in the stereotypes of the poor and working class that have been reinforced by American values. Schools must help children of poverty reveal the causes of their condition and explore the various avenues available to overcome and rewrite these traditional beliefs about their culture.

Chapter 9

Stories of Poverty

Helping people boost themselves out of poverty is the best way to make a lasting positive difference in a person's life.

—Naveen Jain

Public school teachers know more about the struggles of poor families than most people ever will. Each day, they see the damage poverty does to children and how it inhibits their learning. They also see the ill effects of bad parenting, abusive parenting (or no parenting). And they often feel helpless, because there is really so little they can do about many of these situations. But they still try. And many of them make a profound difference in the lives of young children.

• A few years ago, I taught a little boy who had come from another school district. His parents were no longer together and his mom had custody of him and his sister. He was a very friendly and cooperative student with great manners. I noticed right away that he was far behind academically. He also fell asleep in class quite often. I wrote notes to his mom and worked with him in a small group, hoping for improvement. One day I questioned him because he could not read the story he had been assigned for homework. I was very firm and told him he needed to do his homework if we were to see good results. He started crying and in our conversation, told me that they were staying with his aunt and cousins. There were not enough beds so he slept on the sofa. He told me that rats ran along the back of the couch at night and he could not sleep because he was so scared.

I scheduled a conference with his mom and she confirmed that she worked nights, and that they were going through bad times. She cried and cried and felt so bad that she wasn't helping her son. I sent him back to P.E. and talked to her. From my experience of being a single mom, I told her that her little boy needed to see that she was in control and that when I cried, I cried in the shower or when my children were not around. I also asked her if there was a pastor or priest or anyone she could talk to about improving her living arrangements. Last, I wrote down the steps on how she could help her child at home.

It wasn't that she didn't want to. She didn't know how. Long story short, her pastor helped her find a daytime job so she was available to her children at night, and she finally got an apartment for herself. She and her son worked so hard to get him to catch up. He passed second grade and went on to perform at average ability.

• Several years ago, there was a family that someone noticed was living in a home with no electricity. When the school board authorities visited the home, they found that a woman with fourteen children lived there. None of the children were attending school. The older children had been in school at one time but most never went. When questioned, she said she tried to enroll them but didn't know how to get Social Security numbers or birth certificates or fill out the enrollment papers. She had been in special education when younger and could not do it. After the Homeless Department got the children enrolled and paperwork done, one of the children was enrolled in my class. I taught seven- to eight-year-olds in second grade. He was ten years old and had never been in school.

This was quite a challenge for all the teachers who received these children. With a lot of cooperation and hard work, these children learned a lot but did not catch up to their peers. They could not be tested for special education or placed in lower grades because it wasn't their fault that this happened, and it was not fair to label them so soon. Unfortunately, they all moved before the school year ended.

• Cynthia depends on food stamps each month to buy groceries, and she has worked out a system to ensure her family eats well nutritionally. Immediately after she gets her stamps, she rushes out to the supermarket and buys fruits and vegetables, both fresh and frozen, as well as meats and dairy products. Like many of the low-income mothers in the area, Cynthia knows she must buy these types of products with her food stamps because she is sometimes able to supplement her grocery shopping with a monthly trip to her local food pantry, where she is given mainly nonperishable items like pasta, rice, and canned goods. So after her trip to the supermarket, Cynthia seemed to be set for the month. However, Cynthia had gotten behind on her utility bill and she woke up one morning and her power was cut. Knowing the refrigerator was off and the food was going bad, she called the utility company and the Department of Social Services for assistance with getting her power turned back on. By the time the power was restored, the family had lost all of that month's meat, cheese, milk, and other perishable items.

• Jesse Staley is a teenager who dreams of graduating from high school and attending her prom. While her friends buy prom dresses and arrange after-prom parties, she struggles to feed her sisters and brothers. As other families choose between colleges, hers must choose between medical care and welfare. As many of her friends live the life of a carefree adolescent, Jesse assumes the role of the caretaker in her family. The oldest of three children, she must look after her siblings while her father ekes out a living driving a truck. Her father is a hardworking man, but his twelve- to fifteen-hour shifts don't provide enough income to pay the bills. She begins her days early, after her father leaves for work. She wakes up her brother and sister, feeds them, and sends them to school. After attending classes all day, she fixes dinner, helps her siblings with class assignments and puts them to bed—all before starting her own homework. Although the family isn't homeless, they have only 120 dollars each month to buy food. Often, there isn't enough to last the month, so Jessie is forced to turn to charities for help. Her family suffers from the constant struggle to make ends meet. For example, choosing inexpensive over healthy foods has hurt the family's health; Jessie's father has a heart condition and struggles against obesity—the result of high-fat, processed foods that so frequently make up a low-income diet. Jessie's dream of going to college is tempered by fears that her father will need her close to home, especially as he faces growing health problems. It's a sad fact that in America, where there is no universal health coverage, many families face the same terrible choice as Jessie's father between working for a living without health insurance or taking welfare in order to receive state-provided medical care.

• Everything in J.R.'s life changed when his mother became ill and his father had a stroke. Before his parents' illnesses, they had all lived together in a small rented apartment. His mother's poor health forced his dad out of work. When the condition worsened and she moved into a nursing home, J.R. said, "The happiness slowly just went away." Soon after, he and his father lost their apartment, and J.R. entered his first homeless shelter at the age of four. Over the next eleven years, the family went through fourteen different homeless shelters. In one year alone, J.R. switched high schools three times. Homelessness has taken a serious toll on J.R.'s emotional health. "I feel like my childhood was taken away from me," J.R. noted. "I really was neglected in my childhood because I was constantly moving. I was in another shelter and another shelter, another shelter." J.R. felt isolated from other teenagers and, at times, had considered suicide.

• John was a student who never seemed to "get it" in my class. He was not a behavior problem, but he never completed assignments and rarely brought back homework. He was failing the third grade and I was pulling my hair out trying to help him. He seemed to be having trouble seeing the board, so I moved him up front. I am embarrassed to say that in the last six weeks of his third-grade year, the nurse came around for the yearly eye exam. John's eyesight was in the legally blind category. The nurse assisted the family in getting eyeglasses and the last I saw John, he was on the A honor roll!

• A veteran high school English teacher in New Orleans told of a student who had failed kindergarten, suffering from an apparent learning disability. When school officials finally looked at him more closely, they discovered he was deaf, a result of spinal meningitis. The school helped him get hearing aids and by the fourth grade, it was discovered he was actually gifted.

• Keyshawna is 28 and supports her three children on the $12.86 an hour she makes as a nursing assistant attending to people with dementia, Alzheimer's, and brain injuries. She was raised by her father; her mother was addicted to crack cocaine and in and out of her life while she was growing up. Keyshawna had her first child just before turning sixteen, but she still managed to graduate from high school. She later had two other children, each with different fathers; one of them has been sentenced to thirty-six years in state prison for assault and other charges. The family relies on relatives who occasionally buy something the children need, share the grocery bill, or take the children out to eat or to a park. They lived for two years with Keyshawna's sister, before moving to a small, three-bedroom apartment. She would like to move, especially after two gunshot incidents in the neighborhood last summer, but she can't afford to. She tries to protect her children by restricting them to playing near the apartment's front or back doors; she won't let them go to the playground and tells her twelve-year-old son he can't play at a friend's house because there is no parental supervision there.

• "There are nine of us in my family, and we live in a one-bedroom apartment. I share a bunk bed with my sister Judy."

"It's just so stuffed," Judy says. "We don't have enough space for seven kids."

I've seen articles posted on Facebook about how unlikely it is to get out of poverty, how poor people usually stay poor. If I don't get an education, I'll be stuck like my parents.

On the floor we have two mattresses side by side, where three of my other sisters sleep. You have to step toe to heel to get out of the room.

"All we actually need is like a big closet," Judy laughs.

My mom, step-dad and the two youngest ones sleep in the living room.

My mom cleans other people's houses. When she gets home, she keeps on cleaning and takes care of my sisters and brother. I used to think of my family as middle class, but after my parents split up, my mom had four more kids.

"The truth is I haven't looked it up in the dictionary, the word 'poor,'" says my mom, who speaks only Spanish. "To me, poor is when you don't have enough for soup or a roll of toilet paper."

During my freshman year in high school, I wore ripped jeans, and my sneakers had holes in them. It was kind of embarrassing, but I still didn't think I was poor.

I asked my mom to do the math, and she said right now, my family makes $30,000 a year. According to the federal government, we're $15,000 below the poverty line.

That kind of scares me.

But I haven't always been able to make school my priority. When I was younger, I felt like a robot. All I did was go home and help baby sit and clean. I never had that freedom before—to be able to hang out and skate with my friends. So in ninth grade, I started cutting every day.

Then, when I was in the 10th grade, for the second time my mom started asking me if I could stay home from school to watch the kids. If I said no, most of the money she would make would go to a baby sitter.

I failed every class that year. That made me finally realize that if I ever wanted to graduate, I needed to be in school. I switched to a transfer school, and my first trimester, I got perfect attendance. I told my mom I wasn't going to take care of the little ones anymore.

"At first I felt annoyed, like, 'How could this kid dare to say that to me?' My mom says, when I feel that I try my best to give what's necessary. But then I thought about it, and I thought, 'Maybe I'm not doing my job right. I'm not providing enough.'"

Hearing her say that makes me feel selfish, especially since now my sisters are stuck at home every day.

"Sometimes I wish, like, yeah, you would stay home and, like, help," Judy says.

Judy is 14. She and my older sister, Sarahi, who is in college, are always home baby-sitting, cleaning up after my little sisters and helping feed them.

"I don't want to put this all on Mom," Judy says.

Sometimes I feel like I blame my mom too much for having more kids than she could afford. She's always telling us we're lucky because we'll have each other to go to. But when we still had two of our sisters in diapers, and the pregnancy tests came out positive again and again, Judy, Sarahi and I were like, "I'm not washing the bottles this time." Because he's often babysitting his younger siblings and trying to keep his grades up, Jairo hardly has any time to do what he loves—skateboarding.

• Emily Kwong/WNYC

I asked my mom, "Why did she have so many of us?" With each pregnancy, I accepted it and let it happen," she says. "And I felt happy, but I never thought, 'This son I'm gonna have, I'm gonna educate and motivate to become a doctor, or this daughter I'm going to have I'm gonna motivate to become a lawyer.'

"The job of the mother is to feed and clothe them, to give them love, when maybe I didn't have time to give them each enough love," she adds. It gets me mad that my mom works so hard. And there are people out there who are just born into it. They make money like nothing. They don't have to clean houses, wake up early, drain themselves.

I know I should be thinking about going to college when I graduate if I don't want that life, but I'd have to stay at home to afford it. Nine of us in a one-bedroom apartment, no privacy, one bathroom and toys everywhere. I don't know if I can make myself do it.

Now I'm working 13-hour shifts, making food deliveries on a bike. Honestly, I'd rather do that and earn money for my own place. We're told, "If you work hard, you'll get results." But for my family, there haven't been any results—just survival.

These things do not happen to all poverty-stricken families. But each one faces obstacles that make their lives and the lives of their children most difficult. Poverty needs to be addressed, maybe more so than standardized testing. Even with Title I funds, free lunch and breakfast, and free school supplies, the needs of some of these children are not being met.

Chapter 10

Today's Educator

Poverty must not be a bar to learning and learning must offer an escape from poverty.

—Lyndon B. Johnson

Developing a relationship between an adult and a child that positively influences the young person is the single most important action educators can take. It does not matter if the mentoring is through an organized program in which you are matched to a mentee, or if a relationship develops naturally through daily interactions at school, but what do matter are the characteristics of the mentor. Research on people who grew up in poverty and made it to a bachelor's degree showed they all had mentors (Levine and Nidiffer, 1996). Teachers should help all students feel part of a collaborative culture (Payne, 2008).

We need to face the facts: schools will remain ineffective even if every teacher were magnificent because, even though they are enormously important, they are not the only factor involved in determining how well children succeed (Strauss, 2011). One factor is that the stress of living in poverty can impair children's brain development (Noble, McCandliss, and Farah, 2007). Another factor is the formal language used in schools and the fact that school-based language practices must be learned in the context of schooling. Along with all their other tasks, today's teachers must accept the responsibility of teaching students from nondominant groups the language of school.

Teachers have tough new choices to make in today's diverse classrooms. They either must "upgrade" their teaching every year or fall further behind. There is a significant correlation between student achievement and the rate of poverty in the United States, and teachers can make a tremendous impact on the national rate of poverty. Nationally, over seven thousand students a day (1.2 million a year) get so fed up, they drop out. Each dropout costs our economy three-quarters of a million dollars over a lifetime. Imagine the changes in this data one teacher can make.

Many teachers work long hours at school, and some work on weekends. For most, but not all, effort is not an issue. What is an issue is that many still work with the "mental model" of what teaching used to be fifty years ago, based on models they experienced when they were in school. We often see the same "stand and deliver," "kill and drill," and "ability grouping" of kids, oftentimes with desks in a line, reduced movement, little emotional support, and rote memorization building.

If educators wish to successfully conquer the effects of poverty in schools, they must realize that what happens between the first and last bell of each school day is key. Effective twenty-first-century teachers understand that in order to move children of poverty forward, they must help them make connections, validate, respond, educate, and succeed in understanding their choices and how they can impact their lives. It is no secret that many children of poverty arrive at school with different needs from those from wealthier families. They tend to have more medical problems or behavioral issues and often need extra academic help. They do not have such advantages as music lessons, private sports leagues, tutoring, or trips to cultural events, and their schools are left to fill the gaps. "We, as educators, need to step back and stop trying to 'fix' poor students and start addressing ways in which our schools perpetuate classism" (Gorski, 2008).

As an educator, you have the ability to be a huge gift to children living in poverty. In many instances, it is the teacher who makes sure the skills necessary to survive school are carefully taught and mastered, and it is in this gift that changes will occur from one generation to the next. Never has it been more important to give students battling with the culture of poverty this gift (Payne, 2008).

Being tuned into the culture of poverty and being sensitive to the vast array of needs that children of poverty bring to the classroom is a key factor for today's educators. Having this knowledge allows teachers to realize that the social world of school operates by different rules or norms than the social world these children live in. By building warm and caring relationships with these children, teachers will be better able to detect any warning signs that may place children at risk for failure, or interfere with their chances for success in school and in life (Leroy and Symes, 2001). Teachers of impoverished children need to realize that they may be the only dependable and caring adult who is consistent and reliable in their lives of unpredictability and change (Bowman, 1994). It is for this reason that positive and respectful relationships of this nature are so important for these students (Ciaccio, 2000).

Even for those educators that do not believe a poverty-mentality exists, being positive and building on what a student brings to the table can develop a positive, workable plan that can lead to all types of successes for these students. Do not take the effects of thinking positively lightly. This approach causes people to believe in themselves, which is a powerful weapon for students living in poverty. Ignoring this could be quite self-destructive.

The poverty-mentality is based on attitude. It is said to perpetuate poverty because the focus is on what one doesn't have rather than what one does have. Thoughts and comments such as "I can't afford this . . ." and "I'll never have enough money for that . . ." may turn out to be a self-fulfilling prophecy. It's not clear where this concept came from, but one of the earliest motivational speakers to discuss it was Zig Ziglar.

Ziglar noted that focusing on the concern about what is missing in one's life rather than focusing on what is there can lead to further poverty. He also believes that if someone is to break out of poverty and really succeed, they must use what they do have, be grateful for it, and not be jealous of what others may have. It all boils down to an attitude of self-belief and empowerment rather than one of self-pity and jealousy, and this is the best weapon to combat the destructive poverty-mentality.

It is critical that educators plan and prepare for the aspects of poverty by providing emotional support and modeling of how to use their strengths, skills, and knowledge in order to be successful in life (Marlowe and Page, 1999). Utilizing real-life problems in their instructional resources helps impoverished children deal with some of the issues they face. Learning by doing gives students the opportunity to be active and imaginative problem solvers (Bassey, 1996).

An emphasis needs to be made on sparking the desire to learn in children of poverty, which starts with restoring their self-image and encouraging them to see the rewards of schooling. Children will work hard, for intrinsic rewards, only if they have good reasons (Ciaccio, 2000). We need to make them feel that they are loveable, important, and acceptable human beings by making them feel secure and good about themselves and by building trusting relationships with them (Bassey, 1996).

Gorski (2007) reminds us to remember the injustice of living with poverty. The U.S. education system denies students in poverty, in almost every conceivable way, the opportunities and access it affords most wealthier students.

There is no curriculum that will foster resilience in children. Educators need to include coping skills and supportive measures that children in poverty need to survive their challenging environment. If we are to help them adapt successfully, despite adversity, and thrive in spite of negative circumstances, high expectations must be set that communicate guidance, structure, challenge, and most importantly, a belief in the innate resilience of children. In short, we need a curriculum that supports resilience (Benard, 1995).

Most teachers enter the profession to "make a difference," but making a difference can go both ways. If students achieve well, the difference is positive. If students struggle, our nation struggles. Often testing accountability creates doubt in educators, leaving them reconsidering other professions after the first few years teaching.

According to DeWitt (2013), educators have great value in our society:

- The classroom teacher is still the single most significant contributor to student achievement; the effect is greater than that of parents, peers, schools, or poverty.
- The effectiveness of classroom teachers varies dramatically, especially within schools.
- Research shows teachers in the top 20 percent, based on year-to-year progress with their students, will completely erase the effects of academic poverty in five years.
- Most teachers simply don't know how to be a high performer, and others have lost hope and don't try anymore.

The No Child Left Behind policy (2001) requires that all core academic classes be taught by highly qualified teachers. The law also obligates districts and states to ensure that poor and minority children are not taught disproportionately by inexperienced, unqualified, or out-of-field teachers. The result is that high-poverty schools are forced to concentrate on literacy and math to meet testing requirements, while subjects like science and social studies are generally reduced to short vignettes that lack both content and critical thinking.

For students with various cultural and linguistic experiences, it makes sense that the more exposure they have to these aspects, the more resources they have to draw on and support their learning (Dyson, 2003). The emphasis in such classrooms is on what can be done with language rather than what cannot. Good teachers have these opportunities built into their daily routines. The difference between "good" teaching and "poor" teaching accounts for a 30 percent variance in learning. Imagine the impact on variance in learning between good teaching and great teaching.

A good teacher has a focus solely on curriculum and teaching the basics: reading, writing, and arithmetic. Great teachers take this one step further by teaching the whole student. By using nonjudgmental and caring approaches, they acknowledge the child's humanity and understand that they may come to them with their physical and emotional needs unmet. Children of poverty demand great teachers; ones that have broken away from habitual negative-thinking patterns and believe in teaching the child. Schools must become places that teach children to be successful rather than confirm feelings of failure. They must realize that each time they interact with a student, they are programming them how to feel about themselves, and that feeling remains with that child the rest of their life (Helfield, 1997).

STRATEGIES FOR EDUCATORS

Watch the cues:

- Irritable student? Maybe they are hungry.
- Disengaged during class? Maybe they need glasses.
- Asleep at the desk? Maybe they have nightly responsibilities.

Tracking and ability grouping needs to be replaced with higher order pedagogies, innovative learning materials, and holistic teaching and learning. It all starts with demanding basic human rights for all people: adequate housing and health care, living-wage jobs, and so on.

Teachers can help by (Gorski, 2008):

- Educating themselves about class and poverty.
- Rejecting deficit theory—help students and colleagues unlearn misperceptions about poverty.
- Reaching out to low-income families, even when they appear unresponsive.
- Fighting to keep low-income students from being assigned unjustly to special education or low academic tasks.
- Teaching about issues related to class and poverty.
- Fighting to ensure that school meal programs offer healthy options.
- Teaching about the antipoverty work of Martin Luther King Jr., Jane Addams, Cesar Chavez, and other U.S. icons and about why this dimension of their legacies has been erased from national consciousness.
- Making curriculum relevant to poor students, drawing on and validating their experiences and intelligences.
- Never assuming that all students have equal access to such learning resources as computers and the Internet, and never assigning work requiring this access without providing in-school time to complete it.
- Prompting students to reflect on and express their talents, beliefs, and values in assignments and classroom activities. Such personal affirmations can bolster students' confidence and performance and help teachers recognize the unique qualities of all students.

- Avoiding references to free or reduced-price lunches, or other indicators of financial assistance in front of the class. Do not tease about ill-fitting or out-of-style clothing.
- Increasing the number of cooperative learning opportunities. Comparisons and stereotypes are less common in cooperative settings.
- Limiting the use of test scores. Test scores are used to label students, classes, and entire schools as "passing" or "failing." If a students' fate rests on a single test, the likely result over the next few years will be nothing short of catastrophic. Requiring all students to meet the same high standards regardless of family background will inevitably lead to either a large number of failing schools or to a dramatic lowering of state standards; both of which serve to discredit the public education system and lend support to arguments that the system is failing and needs fundamental change like privatization.
- Data from the National Assessment of Educational Progress shows that more than 40 percent of the variation in average reading scores and 46 percent of the variation in average math scores across states is associated with variation in child poverty rates.
- Employing the tenets of Ruby Payne through training for staff on the strategies that effectively work with the student population you serve including:
  a. hidden rules of social cues that differ greatly between the classes;
  b. impact of economic class differences on communication, interaction, and expectations;
  c. symptoms of generational poverty and how they differ from situational poverty;
  d. poverty related behaviors and mindsets that affect learning;
  e. identifications of the resources and strengths of any student; and
  f. tips, tools, and intervention strategies proven to increase teacher effectiveness.

To boost student achievement in high-poverty schools (DeWitt, 2013):

- Relationships still matter, strong relationships and family connections help.
- High expectations are not enough. Help students set crazy high goals and then actively point out to them how their daily actions connect to their long-term goals.
- The most important cognitive skills to build are reasoning, working memory, and vocabulary usage.
- Build academic optimism so that kids hear and believe every day that they can and will succeed. Zero doubt = effort.
- Increase feedback on the learning and zero in on the specifics of effort used, strategies applied, or attitude engaged.

- Engage like crazy using more social collaboration, energizers, participation, and affirmations. When kids feel liked, have goals, and are energized, they work harder.
- Have a positive attitude, or your opinion is useless if you fail to act on it. If and how you act on it is priceless.
- Use hope building and the growth mindset every day, all day.

Before you assign homework, ask yourself:

- Do all my students have a workspace and good lighting to read at home?
- Do my students work in the evening or have household responsibilities?
- Do they have Internet access?
- Is there an adult who can help with homework?

Conclusion

There should be no doubt that there is a profound relationship between poverty and illiteracy. A child's cognitive development and academic performance can be negatively affected by poverty. Combining the additional challenges of limited reading materials, increase in health risks, housing instability, limited food choices, and unsafe environments complicates the fact that they already begin school with 50 percent weaker vocabulary than their wealthier peers.

Unfortunately, most of today's educators are not adequately trained to work with children living in poverty. In order to work with poverty-stricken children, teachers must be involved in every aspect of their life, including personal and academic. Many educators make the mistake of failing to acknowledge the influence poverty can have on a child's life. These children are not always given the foundation they need to succeed in school, such as self-discipline and effective study habits. As they begin to struggle in school, they develop low self-esteem and experience the feeling that they don't belong.

As a result of lower academic performance and reading ability among students in poverty, teachers who are motivated by state accountability often use class time to reinforce reading and test-taking strategies. As opposed to learning real-life problem solving and critical thinking, students are learning obedience, test-taking skills and repetition, things that are not a reality in the life they lead. For the impoverished, achieving a high school diploma is considered an accomplishment. Once obtained, many students choose to attend college, not realizing they do not have the necessary skill set. This results in numerous poverty-stricken students dropping out of college in the first year, due to failing grades, and thus repeating the cycle of poverty.

I am not pointing the finger at teachers. It is often the case in our over-crowded schools that teachers assume the children entering their classroom already have study habits and self-discipline. Nothing could be further from the truth. In a system so driven by testing and scores, teachers often are so overwhelmed with the amount of curriculum that must be covered, there is little time to teach these skills. With the increase in the poverty rate of school-age children, these skills can no longer be ignored; they must be taught. By building close relationships with their students, teachers can model the behaviors necessary to make better choices in their life and instill a sense of well-being.

As Hart and Risley (1997) stated, "In addition to this, there is a profound need to implement and maintain certain programs such as drop-out prevention, tutoring and extra-curricular activities to promote student interest and improve academic achievement and attendance." Regardless whether a school is experiencing 17 percent poverty or 96 percent, it is important that these programs are made available for all students.

Another barrier to student success is the fact that poverty-stricken schools often have high teacher absenteeism, larger class sizes, and increased classroom behavior problems compared to schools with lower poverty levels. Technology access is also a challenge that deprives students the necessary skills to be successful in today's workforce. Textbooks are often limited and outdated, and few contain any acknowledgment of poverty in society. Of the few history textbooks that are available on these campuses, most promote the achievements of affluent people but minimize the poverty-stricken culture of the lower class. It is also unfortunate that, in addition to future educators being ill prepared for working with the impoverished, they are also not armed with a wealth of knowledge to compensate for discrepancies in academic resources, depriving students of the opportunity to learn about cultures similar to their own.

It is so easy to put your head down and deny that poverty levels are as high as they are in America. It is easy even as educators to say that if "they" would only find a job, stay off drugs, or be more involved in their child's education, their impoverished students would succeed. The sad thing is that even if today's teachers do all the suggested things within the pages of this book and proven by research, asking schools to close the achievement gap while ignoring the economic gaps that exist between students growing up in wealth and students growing up in poverty will just result in another national disaster waiting to happen, and our education system will continue to fail our future. You are the only one who can make a change. Start with your classroom and start today.

Terms

Absolute Poverty Line: The threshold below which one is considered to be lacking the financial resources to meet basic needs.

At Risk: Children who are likely to fail in school or in life because of their life's social circumstances.

Classism: Systematic oppression of poor people and people who work for wages by those who have access to control of the necessary resources by which people make their living.

Living Wage: A wage that adequately covers basic needs, taking into account cost of living by area of residence.

Poverty: Lack of adequate resources to be able to provide the basic needs of food, water, clothing, housing, medical care, and education.

References

American Psychological Association (2008). Effects of poverty, hunger and home-lessness on children and youth. Retrieved from http://www.apa.org/pi/families/poverty.aspx.

Bandura, A. (2009). Social cognitive theory of mass communication. In J. Bryant and M. Oliver (eds.), *Media Effects: Advances in Theory and Research*, *3rd Edition* (pp. 94–124). New York: Routledge.

Bassey, M. (1996). Teachers for a changing society: Helping neglected children cope with schooling. *The Educational Forum* 61: 58–62. WilsonWeb, June 30, 2001.

Beaufils, V. (2014). Cracking the class and cultural code. Prezi Presentation. Retrieved from https://prezi.com/p8vb_ov_vuqu/cracking-the-class-cultural-code/.

Beegle, K., Dehejia, R. H., and Gatti, R. (2006). Child labor and agricultural shocks. *Journal of Development Economics* 81: 80–96.

Benard, B. (1995). Fostering resilience in children. ERIC Digests.

Berliner, D. (2012). Inequality, poverty and the widening education gap. School Matters. Retrieved from http://www.schoolsmatter.info/2012/10/david-berliner-on-inequality-poverty.html.

Bernstein, J. (2007). Is education the cure for poverty? *The American Prospect*. Retrieved from http://prospect.org/article/education-cure-poverty.

Books, S. (2004). *Poverty and Schooling in the U.S.: Contexts and Consequences*. Mahwah, NJ: Erlbaum.

Boomer, R., Dworin, J. E., May, L., and Semingson, P. (2008, December). Miseducating Teachers about the poor: A critical analysis of Ruby Payne's claims about poverty. *Teachers College Record* 110(12): 2497–531.

Bourdieu, P. (1997). The forms of capital. In A. H. Halsey, H. Lauder, P. Brown, and A. S. Wells (eds.), *Education: Culture, Economy, and Society* (pp. 40–58). Oxford: Oxford University Press.

Bowman, B. (1994). The challenge of diversity. *Phi Delta Kappan* 76: 234–38. WilsonWeb, July 16, 2001.

Brady-Smith, C., Fauth, R. C., and Brooks-Gunn, J. (1999). Poverty and education—overview, children and adolescents. Retrieved from http://education.stateuniversity.com/pages/2330/Poverty-Education.html.

Brizuela, M., Andersen, E., and Stallings, L. (1999). Discourse markers as indicators of register. *Hispania* 82(1): 128–41.

Brooks-Gunn, J. and Duncan, G. J. (1997). The effects of poverty on children. *Children and Poverty* 7(2): 55–71.

Burgess, A. W., Hartman, C. R., and Clements, P. T. (1995). The biology of memory and childhood trauma. *Journal of Psychosocial Nursing and Mental Health Services* 33(3): 16–26.

Casey, P. (2005). Child health-related quality of life and household food security. *Archives of Pediatrics and Adolescent Medicine* 159: 51–6.

Centers for Disease Control and Prevention (2012). Low level lead exposure harms children; A renewed call for primary prevention. Report of the Advisory committee on childhood lead poisoning prevention. Retrieved from http://www.cdc.gov/nceh/lead/acclpp/final_document_030712.pdf.

Chen, K., Sheth, A., Krejci, J., and Wallace, J. (2003, August). Understanding differences in alcohol use among high school students in two different communities. Paper presented at the annual meeting of the American Sociological Association, Atlanta, GA.

Christenson, S. (2004). The family-school partnership: An opportunity to promote the learning competence of all students. *School Psychology Review* 33: 83–107.

Ciaccio, J. (2000). A teacher's chance for immortality. *The Education Digest* 65(6): 44–8. WilsonWeb, July 16, 2001.

Coleman, J. (1990). *Foundations of Social Theory*. Cambridge, MA: Harvard University Press.

Collins, J. (1988). Language and class in minority education. *Anthropology and Education Quarterly,* 19(4): 299–326.

Compton-Lilly, C. (2004). *Confronting Racism, Poverty and Power; Classroom Strategies to Change the World*. Portsmouth, NH. Heinemann.

Cook, S. C. and Wellman, C. L. (2004). Chronic stress alters dendritic morphology in rat medial prefrontal cortex. *Journal of Neurobiology* 60: 236–48.

Cooper, C., Crosnoe, R., Suizzo, M. A., and Pituch, K. A. (2010). Poverty, race and parental involvement during the transition to elementary school. *Journal of Family Issues* 31: 859.

Covert, B. (2013). Poverty has same effects on brain as constantly pulling all nighters. Think Progress. Retrieved from http://thinkprogress.org/economy/2013/08/30/2555601/living-poverty-effect-brain-constantly-pulling-nighters/.

De Bellis, M. D. (2001). Developmental traumatology: The psychobiological development of maltreated children and its implications for research, treatment, and policy. *Development and Psychopathology* 13: 539–64.

Degenhardt, L., Chiu, W.-T., Sampson, N., Kessler, R. C., Anthony, J. C., Angermeyer, M., Bruffaerts, R., de Girolamo, G., Gureje, O., Huang, Y., Karam, A., Kostyuchenko, S., Lepine, J. P., Mora, M. E. M., Neumark, Y., Ormel, J. H., Pinto-Meza, A., Posada-Villa, J., Stein, D. J., Takeshima, T., and Wells, J. E. (2008). Toward a global view of alcohol, tobacco, cannabis, and cocaine use: Findings from the WHO world mental health surveys. *Public Library of Science Medicine* 5(7): 1053–67.

Delaney-Black V., Covington C., Ondersma S. J., Nordstrom-Klee, B., Templin, T., Ager, J., Janisse, J., and Sokol, R. J. (2002). *Archives of Pediatrics and Adolescent Medicine* 156: 280–85.

Delgado-Gaitan, C. (2004). *Involving Latino Families in Schools: Rising Student Achievement through Home-School partnerships.* Thousand Oaks, CA: Corwin Press.

DeWitt, P. (2013). Five Things most people don't know about poverty and student achievement. *Education Week.* Retrieved from blogs.edweek.org.

Diala, C. C., Muntaner, C., and Walrath, C. (2004). Gender, occupational, and socio-economic correlates of alcohol and drug abuse among U.S. rural, metropolitan, and urban residents. *American Journal of Drug and Alcohol Abuse* 30(2): 409–28.

Driscoll, A. and Nagel, N. G. (2010). *Poverty and the Effects on Children and Parents.* Pearson, Allyn, Bacon, Prentice Hall.

Driscoll, A. and Nagel, N. G. (2012). *Poverty and the Effects on Children and Parents.* Pearson, Allyn, Bacon, Prentice Hall. Retrieved from http://www.education.com.

Duke University School of Medicine (2013). Children who grow up in poverty are more likely to smoke cigarettes. News Medical. Retrieved from http://www.newsmedical.net/news/20130730/Children-who-grow-up-in-poverty-are-more-likely-to-smoke-cigarettes.aspx.

Dyson, A. (2003). Popular literacies and "all" children: Rethinking literacy for contemporary childhoods. *Language Arts,* 81: 100–09.

Evans, C. (2004). Literacy development in deaf students: Case studies in bilingual learning and teaching. *American Annals of the Deaf* 149(1): 17–27.

Fan, X. and Chen, M. (2001). Parental involvement and students' academic achievement: A meta-analysis. *Educational Psychology Review* 13: 1–19.

Feldman, S. (2003). The first teachers. *American Teacher.*

Flessa, J. J. (2007). *Poverty and Education: Toward Effective Action.* Toronto: Elementary Teachers Federation of Ontario.

Ford, J. and Brodsky, A. (2001). The visibility of illicit drugs: Implications community-based drug control strategies. *American Journal of Public Health* 91(12): 1987–1994.

Galea, S., Ahern, J., Tracy, M., and Vlahov, D. (2007). Neighborhood income and income distribution and the use of cigarettes, alcohol, and marijuana. *American Journal of Preventive Medicine* 32(6): S195–S202.

Gee, J. P. (2004). *Situated Language and Learning: A Critique of Traditional Schooling.* New York: Routledge.

Ginsberg, H. and Opper, S. (1969). *Piaget's Theory of Intellectual Development.* Englewood Cliffs, NJ: Prentice-Hall.

Gollnick, D. M., and Chinn, P. C. (2006). *Multicultural Education in a Pluralist Society* (7th edition). Upper Saddle River, NJ: Pearson.

González, N. (2005). Beyond culture: The hybridity of funds of knowledge. In N. González, L. C. Moll, and C. Amanti (eds.), *Funds of Knowledge* (pp. 29–46). Mahwah, NJ: Erlbaum.

Gorski, P. (2008, April). The myth of the culture of poverty. *Educational Leadership* 65(7): 32–6.

Gorski, P. (2012). Perceiving the problem of poverty and schooling: Deconstructing the class stereotypes that mis-shape education practice and policy, *Equity & Excellence in Education* 45(2): 302–19.

Gorski, P. (2007). The questions of class. *Teaching Tolerance*, 31.

Grady, S., Bielick, S., and Aud, S. (2010). *Trends in the Use of School Choice: 1993 to 2007*. Washington, DC: U.S. Department of Education.

Grant, S. D., Oka, E. R., and Baker, J. A. (2009). The culturally relevant assessment of Ebonics-speaking children. *Journal of Applied School Psychology* 25(3): 113–27.

Hart, B. and Risley, T. (1995) Meaningful differences in everyday experience of young American children. Brooks Publishing. Retrieved from http://www.strategiesForchildren.org/eea/6research_summaries/05_meaningfuldifferences.pdf.

Helfield, I. (1997). Is there a difference between good teachers and great ones? *Literacy Across the Curriculumedia Focus*, 16(1): 38.

Hyman, M. (2010). Not having enough food causes obesity and diabetes. Retrieved from http://drhyman.com/blog/2010/09/17/not-having-enough-food-causes-obesity-and-diabetes/.

Irizarry, J. (2009). Characteristics of the cultural deficit model: Alternatives to deficit perspective. Retrieved from www.education.com/refernce/article/cultural-deficit-model/

Jennings, P. K. (2004). What mothers want: Welfare reform and maternal desire. *Journal of Sociology and Social Welfare* 31(3): 113–30.

Kozol, J. (1992). *Savage Inequalities: Children in America's Schools*. New York: HarperCollins.

Kyllonen, P. C. and Gitomer, D. H. (2002). Individual differences. The Gale Group, Inc. Retrieved from www.encyclopedia.com/topic/individual_differences.aspx.

Labbo, L. D., Love, M. S., and Ryan, T. (2007). A vocabulary flood: Making words "sticky" with computer-response activities. *The Reading Teacher* 60: 582–88.

Layton, L. (2013). Study: Poor children are now the majority in American public schools in South, West. *Washington Post*. Retrieved from htpp://www.washingtonpost.com/local/Education/2013/10/16/34eb4984–35bb-11e3–8aOe-4e.

Lee, J. and Bowen, N. K. (2006). Parent involvement, cultural capital, and the achievement gap among elementary school children. *American Educational Research Journal* 43(2): 193–204, 206, 209–18.

Levine, A. and Nidiffer, J. (1996). *Beating the Odds: How the Poor Get to College*. San Francisco: Jossey-Bass.

Li, G. (2010). Race, class, gender, and schooling: Multicultural families doing the hard work of home literacy in America's inner city. *Reading & Writing Quarterly*. Special issue on poverty and reading, by Nathalis Wamba.

Ludy, J., Belden, A., Botteron, K., Marrus, N., Harms, M. P., Babb, C., Nishino, T., and Barch, D. (2013). The effects of poverty on childhood brain development: The mediating effect of caregiving and stress life events. *JAMA Pediatrics* online.

Lupien, S. J., King, S., Meaney, M. J., and McEwen, B. S. (2001). Can poverty get under your skin? Basal cortisol levels and cognitive function in children from low and high socioeconomic status. *Developmental Psychopathology* 13(3): 653–76.

Manza, J. and Sauder, M. (2009). *Inequality and Society: Social Science Perspectives on Social Stratification*. New York: Norton.

Marks, H. (2009). Risk factors for drug addiction and alcoholism. *Everyday Health*. Retrieved from http://www.everydayhealth.com/addiction/drug-addiction-And-alcoholism-risk-factors.aspx.

Marlowe, B. and Page, M. (1999). Making the most of the classroom mosaic: A constructivist perspective. *Multicultural Education* 6(4): 19–21. WilsonWeb, July 10, 2001.

Mayers, S. (1997). *What Money Can't Buy: Family Income and Children's Life Chances*. Cambridge, MA. Harvard University Press.

Miller, G. E. (2015). What is the U.S. poverty line and could you live below it? *20 Something Finance*. Retrieved from http://20somethingfinance.com/what-is-the-united-states-Poverty-line/.

Miller, P. J., Cho, G. E., and Bracey, J. R. (2005). Working-class children's experience through the prism of personal storytelling. *Human Development*, 48, 115–35.

Mills, C. W. (1959). *The Sociological Imagination*. Oxford: Oxford University Press.

Mukherjee, S. (2013). Four ways that poverty hurts Americans' long-term health. *Think Progress*. Retrieved from http://thinkprogress.org/health/2013/07/30/238147/four-ways-poverty-impacts-americans.

National Center for Children in Poverty (2012). *Parental Employment in Low-Income Families*. New York: Author.

National Center for Education Statistics (2005). *Parent and Family Involvement in Education: 2002–2003*. Washington, DC: Author.

National Center on Family Homelessness (2009). *America's Youngest Outcasts 2009: State Report Card on Child Homelessness*. Retrieved from http://www.homeless-childrenamerica.org/pdf/rc_full_report.pdf.

National Council for the Social Studies Professional (2013). Does poverty cause low achievement? Yes—If you look at the big picture. Retrieved from http://www.socialstudies.org/system/files/publications/tssp/TSSP244.pdf.

National Student Campaign Against Hunger and Homelessness (2015). Overview of hunger and homelessness in America. Retrieved from www.studentsagainsthunger.org/page/hhp/Overview-homelessness-america.

Noble, K. G., McCandliss, B. D., and Farah, M. J. (2007). Socioeconomic gradients predict individual differences in neurocognitive abilities. *Developmental Science* 10: 464–80.

Oakes, J. (2006). *Learning Power: Urban Education and Racial Justice*. Second Annual Carnegie Address, Boston College, Chestnut Hill, MA.

Okun, W. (2008). Parents who don't parent. *New York Times*. Retrieved from http:Kristof.blogs.nytimes.com/2008/06/23/parents-who-don't-parent.

Olson, L. (2006). As deadline looms, report says states showing little progress in addressing teacher quality. *Education Week* 25. Retrieved January 29, 2009, from http://www.edweek.org/ew/articles/2006/07/06/42teacherquality_web.h25.html?print=1.

Parramore, L. S. (2014). 11 Jobs where an honest day's work earns you poverty. Retrieved from www.alternet.com/economy/11-jobs-where-honest-days-work-earns-you-poverty.

Payne, R. (2008). Nine powerful practices: Nine strategies help raise the achievement of Students living in poverty. *Educational Leadership*. Association for Supervision and Curriculum Development.

Program for International Student Assessment (2012). PISA 2012 results. Retrieved from http://www.oecd.org/pisa/keyfindings/pisa-2012-results.htm.

Pyke, A. (2013). Growing up poor changes children's brains and may even shorten their lives. *Think Progress*. Retrieved from http://thinkprogress.org/economy/2013/10/22/2816021/Poverty-childrens-brains.

Rothstein, R. (2013). Does poverty cause low achievement? The Economic Policy Institute. Retrieved from http://www.epi.org/blog/poverty-achievement.

Saxe, L., Kadushin, C., Beveridge, A., Livert, D., Tighe, E., Rindskopf, D., Schore, A. (2002). Advances in neuropsychoanalysis, attachment theory, and trauma research: Implications for self-psychology. *Psychoanalytic Inquiry* 22: 433–84.

Schore, A. N. (2002). Dysregulation of the right brain: A fundamental mechanism of traumatic attachment and the psychopathogenesis of posttraumatic stress disorder. *Australian and New Zealand Journal of Psychiatry* 36: 9–30.

Shanks, T. R. (2012). For poor children, trying hard is not enough. *CNN iReport*. Retrieved from http://edition.cnn.com/2012/07/12/opinion/Shanks-education.

Speicher, B. L., and Bielanski, J. R. (2000). Critical thoughts on teaching standard English. *Curriculum Inquiry* 30(2): 147–69.

Steele, C. M. (2010). *Whistling Vivaldi: And Other Clues to How Stereotypes Affect Us*. New York: Norton.

Stipek, D. (2004). Teaching practices in kindergarten and first grade: Different strokes for different folks. *Early Childhood Research Quarterly* 19(4): 548–68.

Strauss, V. (2011). Public education's biggest problem gets worse. The Answer Sheet. Retrieved from http://Washingtonpost.com/blogs/answer-sheet/post/

Templeton, D. (2013). Evidence mounting that poverty causes lasting physical and mental health problems for children. *Pittsburg Post Gazette*. Retrieved from http://www.post-gazette.com/news/healthy2013/11/25/children-and-poverty/stories/201311250024.print.

Terry, N. P. and Irving, M. A. (2010). Cultural and linguistic diversity: Issues in Education. In Colarusso, R. P. and O'Rourke, C. M. (eds.), *Special Education for All Teachers*. 5th edition. Dubuque, IA: Kendall Hunt. Retrieved from https://www.kendallhunt.com/uploadedFiles/Kendall_Hunt/Content/Higher_Education/Uploads/Colarusso_CH04_5e.pdf.

Trotman, M. F. (2001). Involving the African American parent: Recommendations to increase the level of parent involvement within African American families. *The Journal of Negro Education* 70(4): 275–86.

U.S. Census Bureau (2000). The survey of income and program participation. U.S. Department of Commerce.

U.S. Department of Agriculture (2009). Access to affordable and nutritious food. Economic Research Service Report Summary. Retrieved from http://www.ers.usda.gov/media/242654/ap036_reportsummary_1_.pdf.

West-Olatunji, C., and Conwill, W. (2010). *Counseling African Americans,* a book in the Supplementary Monograph Series to accompany D. Choudhuri, A. L. Santiago-Rivera, and M. Garrett, *Multicultural Counseling Competency*. Boston: Houghlin Mifflin.

Wilson, W. J. (1997). *When Work Disappears*. New York: Random House.

Worstall, T. (2013). 29 uncomfortable myths about soaring poverty in America. *Forbes*. Retrieved from http://www.forbes.com/sites/timworstall/2013/10/29/29.

www.ingramcontent.com/pod-product-compliance
Lightning Source LLC
Chambersburg PA
CBHW020358270326
41926CB00007B/498